The Workplace Violence Prevention Handbook

Don Philpott and Don Grimme

GOVERNMENT INSTITUTES
An imprint of
The Scarecrow Press, Inc.
Lanham, Maryland • Toronto • Plymouth, UK
2009

 **Government Institutes**

Published in the United States of America
by Government Institutes, an imprint of The Scarecrow Press, Inc.
A wholly owned subsidary of
The Rowman & Littlefield Publishing Group, Inc.
4501 Forbes Boulevard, Suite 200
Lanham, Maryland 20706
http://www.govinstpress.com/

Estover Road
Plymouth PL6 7PY
United Kingdom

Copyright © 2009 by Government Institutes

British Library Cataloguing in Publication Information Available

Library of Congress Cataloging-in-Publication Data

Philpott, Don, 1946–
    The workplace violence prevention handbook / Don Philpott and Don Grimme.
        p. cm.
    Includes bibliographical references and index.
    ISBN: 978-1-60590-646-1 (hbk : alk. paper) — ISBN 978-60590-668-3 (pbk. : alk. paper) —
ISBN 978-1-60590-647-8 (electronic)
    1. Violence in the workplace—United States—Prevention. 2. Violence in the workplace—
United States. I. Grimme, Don. II. Title.
    HF5549.5.E43P49 2009
    658.3'8—dc22   2009008626

♾™ The paper used in this publication meets the minimum requirements of
American National Standard for Information Sciences—Permanence of
Paper for Printed Library Materials, ANSI/NISO Z39.48-1992.
Manufactured in the United States of America.

Contents

Introduction

The terrorist attacks that occurred in New York, Washington, D.C., and Pennsylvania on September 11, 2001, were a tragic reminder to the nation of the danger posed by international terrorism. With the exception of the attack on the Pentagon, the targets chosen by the terrorists were not military in nature, and all were workplaces where thousands of people work every day to support their families and their country.

Thus 9/11 became a huge wake-up call for Americans to the danger of organized terrorism. But most of us have yet to wake up to what may be an even greater danger, certainly a more chronic one: that of unorganized terrorism—those so-called random acts of violence that have been plaguing this nation (and especially this nation) for years. For example, in the introduction to *The Gift of Fear*, author Gavin de Becker observes that in a recent two-year period, "more Americans died from gunshot wounds . . . than were killed during the entire Vietnam War. In contrast, in all of Japan . . . the number of young men shot to death in a year is equal to the number killed in New York City in a single busy weekend."

Workplace violence is violence or the threat of violence against workers. It can occur at or outside the workplace and can range from threats and verbal abuse to physical assaults and homicide, which is one of the leading causes of

We're not sure why de Becker chooses to focus on young men. But his particular comparison happens to have special meaning for one of the authors, when he was a young man. The closest that coauthor Don Grimme ever came to being violently killed was not during his military service in Vietnam, but one year later, while working for an employment agency on the top floor of an office building in the heart of midtown Manhattan. Read more about this in Step 3.

job-related deaths. However it manifests itself, workplace violence is a growing concern for employers and employees nationwide.

The National Institute for Occupational Safety and Health (NIOSH) found that an average of twenty workers are murdered each week in the United States. In addition, an estimated one million workers are victims of nonfatal workplace assaults each year. That's an average of eighteen thousand assaults every week.

Mass murders on the job by disgruntled employees are media-intensive events. However, these mass murders, while serious, are relatively infrequent events. It is the threats, harassment, bullying, domestic violence, stalking, emotional abuse, intimidation, and other forms of behavior and physical violence that, if left unchecked, may result in more serious violent behavior. These are the behaviors that supervisors and managers have to deal with every day, because employers are responsible for providing a safe and healthful workplace for their employees.

"Workplace Violence on the Upswing"

This was the headline of a July 2005 *HR Magazine* article by Kathy Gurchiek, which asserted, "Workplace violence has increased over the past two years despite federal statistics to the contrary." Why the discrepancy? Because they are looking at different phenomena.

Federal statistics focus on physical attacks, which have declined somewhat during the past several years, especially homicides.

The Risk Control Strategies survey used by the *HR Magazine* article focuses on other forms of violence:

- verbal and electronic threats
- sexual harassment
- malicious downloading of viruses

As you will see, these definitely have been on the increase.

Workplace violence has become a serious occupational health problem requiring the combined efforts of employers, employees, labor unions, government, academic researchers, and security professionals. The problem cannot be solved by government alone.

What can be done to prevent workplace violence? Any preventive measure must be based on a thorough understanding of the risk factors associated with the various types of workplace violence. And even though our understanding of the factors that lead to workplace violence is not perfect, sufficient information is available that, if utilized effectively, can reduce the risk. Understanding alone is not sufficient, however. Strong management commitment and the day-to-day involvement of managers, supervisors, employees, and labor unions are also required.

The best protection employers can offer is to establish a zero-tolerance policy toward violence against or by their employees. The employer should establish a violence prevention program or incorporate the information into an existing accident prevention program, employee handbook, or manual of standard operating procedures. It is critical to ensure that all employees know the policy and understand that all claims of workplace violence will be investigated and remedied promptly.

How This Book Is Organized

This book provides a five-step process for understanding and preventing workplace violence. It looks at the extent of the problem; examines some of the myths surrounding it; and provides early warning and detection signs, best prevention policies, and proven defusing, protection, and containment techniques and strategies. At the end of each section is a combination of case studies, scenarios, worksheets, and checklists to assist you in understanding the steps needed to plan, develop, and execute an effective workplace violence prevention program.

The Five-Step Process

The goal of implementing workplace violence protection policies and programs is to make all the nation's workplaces—from schools to offices and hospitals to late-night convenience stores—safer places for both those who work there and those who visit. A safer workplace is a more secure workplace, and this helps boost morale and well-being.

The aim of this handbook is to make all of our working environments safer places in which to work, while at the same time maintaining the quality of life that we have come to expect over many years.

In order to develop a workplace violence prevention plan you have to know the nature of the problem, the extent of the problem, whom you are protecting, and how vulnerable they are. You have to know where any threats might come from and what you can do to prevent them or mitigate them. You need to be aware of all the options available to you. Armed with this knowledge, you can develop and implement the most appropriate plan for your workplace.

The five-step process enables you to understand the different elements that need to be considered when developing your workplace violence prevention program. These five steps are as follows: (1) understand, (2) detect, (3) defuse and protect, (4) assess and contain, and (5) prevent.

STEP 1: UNDERSTAND

Understanding the nature and scope of workplace violence is the foundation of developing an effective strategy to prevent it. Workplace violence ranges from a disgruntled employee bursting in with a shotgun and blasting his colleagues to more subtle forms of violence such as sexual harassment and cyberbullying. All workplace violence is insidious, and steps must be taken to prevent it. The worst mistake a manager can make is to say: "It can't happen here." It can and probably will—and you must be prepared for it.

STEP 2: DETECT

Recognizing warning signs, unusual behavior, and triggering events is critical for both employers and employees in preempting workplace violence. Indicators of increased risk of violent behavior are available and should be utilized to identify potential threats from existing employees, when hiring new ones, and when interacting with customers and strangers.

STEP 3: DEFUSE AND PROTECT

It is impossible to predict with certainty if and when someone—especially an outsider—may become violent, so it is important that everyone know how best to defuse a hostile person or threatening situation. This involves training. There are also many other actions that management can take to make the workplace as secure as possible. These include physical security measures such as access controls and identity cards, and closed-circuit TV and enhanced lighting in parking lots for employees who work late shifts. It may also include the use of security professionals, who will need to be properly trained.

STEP 4: ASSESS AND CONTAIN

This step includes the measures that management can take to put in place the policies and procedures to prevent workplace violence. It covers the risk assessment and incident response teams—how to choose the right team members, what their roles are, and how they should conduct a risk assessment and develop an incident response plan. This plan should include detailed protocols for containment in the event of an incident, evacuation procedures, and communications policies. It should also contain post-event protocols such as notifying authorities, providing support to victims and employees, and analyzing and revisiting the incident response plan and workplace violence prevention program to determine what changes may be necessary.

STEP 5: PREVENT

The final step brings all the above steps together and contains the preventive measures that can be taken to prevent violence from scarring your workplace. It includes how to ensure that your workplace is not a breeding ground for violence, developing company policies on violence and weapons in the workplace, and utilizing proper discipline and termination procedures and employee selection procedures and techniques. It addresses reporting procedures and management and employee training. To assist you in your planning, we include a number of sample templates for policies, procedures, and incident logs, as well as checklists that you can use.

Putting It All Together

When developing a workplace violence prevention plan and instituting policies, it is important to take into account each of the steps above, and especially the relationship between them. A model plan is one in which everyone knows why the program is in place and what their responsibilities are.

As you go through this handbook, you will notice a lot of different levels of detail. It is your choice how deep you want to go, and that will depend on a number of factors. These include how much you already know, the level of risk to your workplace, and what plans and policies are already in place.

A workplace violence prevention plan is a must. Apart from the legal and liability issues, it just makes sense to protect the organization's most valuable assets—the workforce. For many organizations there are added benefits from implementing a violence prevention plan. During the risk assessment phase, you frequently discover areas of vulnerability that can be remedied and practices that can be improved. This may lead to increased productivity and efficiency, which could have an ongoing impact on your bottom line. The biggest benefit, however, is in increased safety for everyone using the workplace.

Understand

Clearly, violence in the workplace affects society as a whole. The economic cost, difficult to measure with any precision, is certainly substantial. There are intangible costs, too. Like all violent crime, workplace violence creates ripples that go beyond what is done to a particular victim. It damages trust, community, and the sense of security every worker has a right to feel while on the job. In that sense, everyone loses when a violent act takes place, and everyone has a stake in efforts to stop violence from happening.

Two Myths

During the years we have been consulting on this issue, we've observed two prevailing myths regarding workplace violence.

MYTH 1: "IT CAN'T HAPPEN HERE."

We call this myth the ostrich syndrome. If the wave of violence over the past several years has demonstrated anything, it is that violence can strike at any time, in any community, in any workplace. The era of workplace violence began in 1986, when postal worker Patrick Sherrill murdered fourteen coworkers in Edmond, Oklahoma—at the time, the third worst mass murder in U.S. history. According to the Federal Bureau of Investigation's 2004 report, *Workplace Violence*:

> Though the most deadly, the Edmond tragedy was not the first episode of its kind in this period. In just the previous three years, four postal employees had been killed by present or former coworkers in separate shootings in Johnston, South Carolina; Anniston, Alabama; and Atlanta, Georgia.

But it's not just post offices. More recently we've seen violence assault a high school in Littleton, Colorado; two day-trading firms in Atlanta; Xerox in Honolulu; a small software firm outside of Boston; Lockheed Martin in Mississippi; and a university in rural Virginia (the worst civilian gun massacre in U.S. history). And in June 2008, five coworkers were killed in a shooting rampage in Henderson, Kentucky.

But are these just isolated incidents? Let's take a look:

- The Centers for Disease Control and Prevention have declared workplace violence to be at epidemic levels.
- The U.S. Department of Justice proclaimed the workplace to be the most dangerous place in America.
- In fact, one in four workers is attacked, threatened, or harassed every year.

Note that, according to *Report of the United States Postal Service Commission on a Safe and Secure Workplace*, quoted in U.S. Postal Service Annual Report for 2000 and in FBI's *Workplace Violence*: "Despite a number of highly publicized post office incidents, a Postal Service commission reported in 2000 that postal employees are actually less likely to be homicide victims than other workers. The phrase 'going postal,' which the commission noted has become a pejorative shorthand phrase for employee violence, is a 'myth,' the report said."

The effects of violence can range in intensity and include the following:

- minor physical injuries
- serious physical injuries
- temporary or permanent physical disability
- psychological trauma
- death

And the toll this violence is taking? Costs related to workplace violence have risen a staggering 2,881 percent—from $4.2 billion in 1992 to $121 billion in 2002, according to *HR Magazine*.

Violence may also have negative organizational outcomes such as low worker morale, increased job stress, increased worker turnover, reduced trust of management and coworkers, and a hostile working environment.

All right, that's the bad news. The good news is revealed when we expose Myth 2.

MYTH 2: "IT CAN'T BE PREVENTED."

Balderdash! In fact, 99 percent of incidents have clear warning signs—if you know what to look for. The extensive news reports of the massacre at Virginia

Tech in 2007 did a pretty good job identifying Seung-Hui Cho's warning signs. The entry on Cho in Wikipedia includes an excellent description of the warning signs exhibited by Cho; we use him as one of our examples in Step 2. But let's look now at another example.

Within just hours of the Lockheed-Martin murders in Mississippi in 2003, reporters learned that the gunman had had frequent conflicts with managers and coworkers. He was a known racist and talked about killing people. You don't have to be a forensic psychologist to detect warning signs like that.

We'll explore the warning signs of violence in much greater depth in Step 2. But now . . .

A Quiz

1. True or False: Domestic violence has little impact on workplace violence.
2. True or False: Homicide is the leading cause of on-the-job death for women.
3. Each year the number of victims of workplace violence is about
   - ❏ 50,000
   - ❏ 100,000
   - ❏ 500,000
   - ❏ 1 million
4. In the workplace, simple assaults outnumber homicides by a factor of
   - ❏ 10 to 1
   - ❏ 50 to 1
   - ❏ 100 to 1
   - ❏ 600 to 1
5. The person most likely to attack someone in the workplace would be a
   - ❏ customer
   - ❏ stranger
   - ❏ coworker
   - ❏ boss
   - ❏ former employee

The Nature and Scope of Workplace Violence

We used the format of the quiz to present the true nature and scope of the problem. Here are the correct answers:

1. False. In fact, domestic violence spillover is the fastest-growing category of physical workplace violence. Each year, about one million women become victims of violence at the hands of an intimate—a husband, boyfriend, or

ex-boyfriend. Some estimates are even higher. According to the U.S. Bureau of Justice, women are about six times more likely than men to experience violence committed by an intimate. When an employee is the target of an attack in the workplace by an intimate, other employees may also be placed at risk.

2. True. Homicide is the leading cause of on-the-job death for women. And it's second only to motor vehicle crashes as the leading cause for men. However, men are at three times higher risk of becoming victims of workplace homicides than women. The majority of workplace homicides are robbery-related crimes (71 percent), with only 9 percent committed by coworkers or former coworkers. Additionally, 76 percent of all workplace homicides are committed with a firearm.

3. One million victims of workplace violence annually. And we're just talking about physical violence. Some estimates are as high as two million. The problem with getting a more accurate number is that most nonlethal workplace violence is never reported to the police. But, of course, not all workplace violence is homicides.

4. In the workplace, simple assaults outnumber homicides by a factor of 600 to 1. The point here is that there are less than one thousand workplace homicides each year. And homicides have been declining during the past few years. However, these homicides, which understandably receive all the media coverage, are only the tip of the iceberg of total workplace violence, which also includes rapes, robberies, and assaults (both with and without a weapon). (See figure 1.1.)

   Nonfatal workplace assaults result in more than 876,000 lost workdays and $16 million in lost wages. Nonfatal assaults occur among men and women at an almost equal rate. And notice that the incidence of verbal violence—threats, intimidation, and harassment—is at least six times that of physical violence. This includes bullying, another major problem in the workplace. Bullying is estimated to affect one-fifth of the U.S. workforce (21 percent, according to a 2001 University of Michigan survey).

   Also, as stated previously, the newest form of workplace violence is electronic: e-mailed threats, computer tampering, and malicious downloading of viruses are very much on the increase.

5. If you thought the person most likely to attack someone in the workplace would be a former employee or coworker, that's understandable, based on press coverage. However, the correct answer is customer—at about 44 percent. For example, perpetrator Mark Barton was a customer, not an employee, of those Atlanta day-trading firms. And, as a student, Seung-Hui Cho was a customer of Virginia Tech.

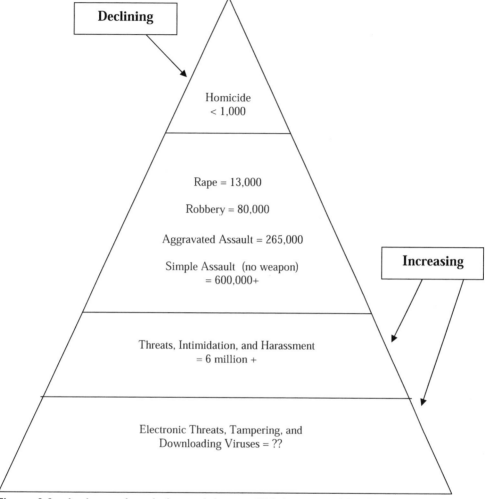

Declining

Homicide
< 1,000

Rape = 13,000

Robbery = 80,000

Aggravated Assault = 265,000

Simple Assault (no weapon)
= 600,000+

Increasing

Threats, Intimidation, and Harassment
= 6 million +

Electronic Threats, Tampering, and
Downloading Viruses = ??

Figure 1.1. Iceburg of workplace violence. ("Violence and Theft in the Workplace," Bureau of Justice Statistics—U.S. Department of Justice, http://www.ojp.usdoj.gov/bjs/pub/press/thefwork.pr; "Workplace Violence, 1992-96," Bureau of Justice Statistics—U.S. Department of Justice, http://www.ojp.usdoj.gov/bjs/abstract/wv96.htm; and "Violence in the Workplace," NIOSH, http://www.cdc.gov/niosh/violcont.html.)

You would get partial credit if you answered "stranger," which is the most likely perpetrator of workplace homicides and, at 24 percent, second only to customers for total workplace violence.

Former employees cause only 3 percent of workplace attacks. Current employees—that is, coworkers—are a more significant source at 20 percent. Bosses are responsible for 7 percent of all physical workplace violence.

Bear in mind, however, that these statistics are based on reported incidents. As we mentioned, most employee fistfights and shovings go unreported.

Types of Workplace Violence and Their Characteristics

Workplace violence occurs in a variety of forms. These types are violence by strangers, violence by customers or clients, violence by coworkers, violence by personal relations, and violence by terrorism. These types of workplace violence and their specific characteristics are described below:

TYPE 1: VIOLENCE BY STRANGERS

Violence by strangers involves verbal threats, threatening behavior, or physical assaults by an assailant who has no legitimate business relationship to the workplace. The person enters the affected workplace to commit a robbery or criminal act. Violence by strangers is responsible for the majority of fatal injuries related to workplace violence nationally. Workplaces at risk of violence by strangers commonly include late-night retail establishments and taxicabs.

TYPE 2: VIOLENCE BY CUSTOMERS OR CLIENTS

Violence by customers or clients involves verbal threats, threatening behavior, or physical assaults by an assailant who either receives services from or is under the custodial supervision of the affected workplace or the victim. Assailants can be current or former customers or clients such as passengers, patients, students, inmates, criminal suspects, or prisoners. The workers at risk typically provide services to the public, such as municipal bus or railway drivers, health care and social service providers, teachers, sales personnel, and other public or private sector service employees. Law enforcement personnel are also at risk of assault, for example, from individuals over whom they exert custodial supervision. Violence by customers or clients may occur on a daily basis in certain industries.

It is pertinent to further illustrate violence by customers or clients with two special cases. The first involves individuals that may have a history of violent behavior, such as prison inmates and mental health service recipients. Situations where this may occur are usually well recognized, and prevention focuses on appropriate staffing and specialized training, augmented with other control measures. The second arises when clients or customers may be "situationally" violent and are provoked when they become frustrated by delays or by the denial of benefits or social services. In these cases, problem anticipation, appropriate training, and other control measures deemed effective are the focus of prevention.

TYPE 3: VIOLENCE BY COWORKERS

Violence by coworkers involves verbal threats, threatening behavior, or physical assaults by an assailant who has some employment-related involvement with the workplace—a current or former employee, supervisor, or manager, for example. In committing a threat or assault, the individual may be seeking revenge for what is perceived as unfair treatment. This type of violence accounts for a much smaller proportion of the fatal workplace injuries than violence by strangers.

TYPE 4: VIOLENCE BY PERSONAL RELATIONS

Violence by personal relations involves verbal threats, threatening behavior or physical assaults by an assailant who, in the workplace, confronts an individual with whom he or she has or had a personal relationship outside of work. Personal relations include a current or former spouse, lover, relative, friend, or acquaintance. The assailant's actions are motivated by perceived difficulties in the relationship or by psychosocial factors that are specific to the assailant.

Domestic violence is one component of this type of workplace violence: violence by a domestic partner or arising from another personal relationship that then follows someone to work. Domestic violence is a pattern of behavior in which one intimate partner uses physical violence, coercion, threats, intimidation, isolation, and emotional, sexual, or economic abuse to control the other partner in a relationship. Stalking or other harassing behavior is often an integral part of domestic violence. Domestic violence is a serious problem that affects people from all walks of life. It can adversely affect the well-being and productivity of employees who are victims, as well as their coworkers. Other effects of domestic violence in the workplace include increased absenteeism, turnover, health care costs, and reduced productivity.

> Remember: Homicide is by far the most frequent manner in which women workers are fatally injured at work.

TYPE 5: VIOLENCE BY TERRORISM

Violence by terrorism is not the same as Type 1 (violence by strangers) because with terrorism the building is often the target rather than the people working in it. However, if a terrorist plants a bomb in a building or releases deadly anthrax spores, workers are killed and maimed. Today, this is a very real danger.

Terrorists usually target high-profile buildings such as national landmarks or major federal or commercial centers. However, as their aim is to cause maximum chaos, many other facilities are at immediate risk, such as nuclear and chemical plants, food processing plants, and water treatment works. Just because your workplace does not fall under one of these categories, it does not

WORKPLACE VIOLENCE

Homicides
Rapes
Robberies
Aggravated assaults
Simple assaults
Bullying, threats, and intimidation
Harassment
Electronic (threatening e-mails, computer sabotage, downloading viruses)

mean that this is something that doesn't concern you. For instance, if you work opposite a federal building that is a terrorist's target, what would be the impact on you and your workplace if a massive bomb exploded just yards away? What would happen if a chemical plant across town was sabotaged and the flume of poisonous gases was being blown in your direction?

While the risk of a terrorist attack is thankfully low, the chance of an attack cannot be ruled out. At the very least, it has to be planned for and policies and procedures must be put in place—and practiced—in order to prevent or miti-gate such an eventuality.

Who Is Vulnerable?

- Men certainly are vulnerable (twice as likely as women), but remember that murder is the number one cause of workplace death for women.
- Supervisors and managers are; during a recent ten-year period, employee-boss murders doubled.
- Occupations like law enforcement officers, taxi drivers, health care and retail workers, and departments like security, safety, and Human Resources (HR) are especially at risk.
- In general, anyone working a job that involves extensive contact with the public or with employees is vulnerable.

These are highlights of those people most vulnerable to lethal violence. Anyone is vulnerable to nonlethal violence.

Workplace violence can strike anywhere, and no one is immune. Some work-ers, however, are at increased risk. Among them are workers who exchange money with the public; deliver passengers, goods, or services; or work alone or in small groups, during late night or early morning hours, in high-crime areas, or in community settings and homes where they have extensive contact with the public. This group includes health care and social service workers such as visiting nurses, psychiatric evaluators, and probation officers; community workers such as gas and water utility employees, phone and cable TV installers, and letter carriers; retail workers; and taxi drivers. According to the FBI report on workplace violence:

> Type 1 violence by criminals otherwise unconnected to the workplace accounts for the vast majority—nearly 80 percent—of workplace homicides. In these incidents, the motive is usually theft, and in a great many cases, the criminal is carrying a gun or other weapon, increasing the likelihood that the victim will be killed or seriously wounded. This type of violence falls heavily on particular occupational groups whose jobs make them vulnerable: taxi drivers (the job that carries by far the highest risk of being murdered), late-night retail or gas station clerks, and others who are on duty at night, who work in isolated locations or dangerous neighborhoods, and who carry or have access to cash.

Law enforcement personnel are at risk of assault from the "object" of public safety services (suspicious persons, detainees, or arrestees) when making arrests, conducting drug raids, responding to calls involving robberies or domestic disputes, serving warrants and eviction notices, and investigating suspicious vehicles. Similarly, correctional personnel are at risk of assault while guarding or transporting jail or prison inmates. According to the FBI:

> Type 2 cases typically involve assaults on an employee by a customer, patient, or someone else receiving a service. In general, the violent acts occur as workers are performing their normal tasks. In some occupations, dealing with dangerous people is inherent in the job, as in the case of a police officer, correctional officer, security guard, or mental health worker. For other occupations, violent reactions by a customer or client are unpredictable; they may be triggered by an argument, anger at the quality of service or denial of service, delays, or some other precipitating event.
>
> Employees experiencing the largest number of Type 2 assaults are those in health-care occupations—nurses in particular, as well as doctors, nurses, and aides who deal with psychiatric patients; members of emergency medical response teams; and hospital employees working in admissions, emergency rooms, and crisis or acute care units.

Any workplace can be at risk of violence by a coworker or personal relation. The FBI report classifies these as Type 3 and Type 4 incidents:

> Type 3 and Type 4 violence are incidents involving violence by past or present employees and acts committed by domestic abusers or arising from other personal relationships that follow an employee into the workplace.

Thus far in the United States, victimization by terrorism, Type 5 violence, has occurred quite infrequently, albeit dramatically and tragically. Terrorist attacks have been a critical rather than a chronic condition. Those working in major metropolitan areas, for government agencies, or employed in critical infrastructure facilities probably are at greatest risk.

Is Your Workplace a Breeding Ground for Violence?

While workplace violence has been around for generations, the systematic mistreatment of employees by colleagues and superiors has only recently been in focus in the United States (see Charlotte Rayner and L. Keashly, "Bullying at Work," in *Counterproductive Workplace Behavior*, edited by S. Fox and P. Spector, 2004). And while people are ultimately responsible for causing violent behavior, bad working environments and practices can be contributory factors.

Charlotte Rayner, in "Reforming Abusive Organizations" (in *Workplace Violence: Issues, Trends, and Strategies*, edited by Vaughan Bowie, Bonnie Fisher, and Cary Cooper), highlights two potential breeding grounds:

1. negative interpersonal behavior—for example, bullying and harassment
2. negative organizational behavior—that is, systems and processes that fail to support, undermine, or otherwise cause harm to employees

Underpinning both are repeated experiences (a sequence of often small events that persist over time) and escalating conflict.

NEGATIVE INTERPERSONAL BEHAVIOR

Emotional abuse, harassment at work, and victimization at work are major problems. Up to 10 percent of the workforce may be victims of this at any one time, according to S. Einarsen et al. in "Workplace Bullying: Individual Pathology or Organizational Culture?" (in *Workplace Violence: Issues, Trends, and Strategies*).

In September 2007, Zogby International conducted the largest national scientific survey into workplace bullying for the Workplace Bullying Institute (www .bullyinginstitute.org). The key findings were as follows:

- Workplace bullying is an epidemic.
  Thirty-seven percent of American workers, an estimated 54 million people, have been bullied at work. It affects half (49 percent) of American workers, 71.5 million workers, when witnesses are included.
- Bullying is same-gender/same-race harassment ignored by current laws.
  Bullying is four times more prevalent than illegal forms of "harassment."
- American employers can and do ignore bullying.
  In 62 percent of the cases, when made aware of bullying, employers worsen the problem or simply do nothing, despite losing an estimated 21–28 million

workers because of bullying. (The Workplace Bullying Institute—Legislative Campaign at workplacebullyinglaw.org is attempting to effect anti-bullying state laws. Thirteen states have introduced the WBI Healthy Workplace Bill since 2003.)

- Most bullies are bosses—the stereotype is real.
  Seventy-two percent of bullies are bosses. Fifty-five percent of those bullied are rank-and-file workers.
- Bullying most strongly affects women.
  Women are targeted by bullies more frequently (in 57 percent of cases), especially by other women (in 71 percent of cases).
- Bullying is a public health hazard.
  For 45 percent of bullied targets, stress affects their health. Thirty-three percent suffer for more than one year.
- Bullied individuals are not "sue crazy"; many fail to even complain.
  Only 3 percent of bullied targets file lawsuits. Forty percent never complain.
- Perpetrators suffer little despite inflicting suffering.
  Targets have to stop the vast majority of bullying (77 percent) by losing their jobs, despite being the ones harmed.

To read the complete report, go to bullyinginstitute.org/zogby2007/wbi-zogby2007.html.

NEGATIVE ORGANIZATIONAL BEHAVIOR

The Safest Organizational Culture Is an Open Culture

Organizational cultures that discourage communication, foster stress, and suppress positive attitudes are breeding grounds for the full range of violent acts that can be committed in the workplace.

> In order to prevent workplace violence, it is critical to embrace open communication and encourage feedback from your employees. Communicating strong organizational values helps set the tone of what your company expects from everyone. When the culture supports a zero tolerance policy towards violence, intimidation and threats, employees become more comfortable with attacking the signs of potential violence and less tolerant of its effects. (See "Workplace Violence: It Occurs More Often Than You Imagine," www.lazorpoint.com/experience/gm_WorkplaceViolence.asp.)

It is important to remember that even the most respectful environment can experience incidents of workplace violence. The environment may not always be the stressor that leads to the occurrence of an incident. An employee may be experiencing psychological problems, be under the influence of alcohol or drugs, or be suffering from familial stress. He or she may have developed a "romantic" obsession for another employee, feeling abandoned and humiliated

Office Rage

Stressful working conditions—coupled with downsizing, outsourcing, and reengineering efforts—have nurtured environments receptive to incidents of workplace violence. Downsizing initiatives and increased workload responsibilities ("do more with less") have replaced the job-for-life security once enjoyed by the workforce.

This new employee insecurity has caused an increase in stress-related illnesses. As the number of jobs decreases, competition and tensions among workers increase. Success on the job is often measured by promotions. However, the opportunity for promotions dwindles in a downsized environment, causing more stress and anxiety. Between 1981 and 1990, a period marked by outsourcing initiatives and force reductions, the number of compensation claims submitted by federal civil servants for emotional illnesses rose more than fourfold.

To make matters worse, some bureaucrats still "rule" their organizations with an iron fist. Decisions are often made in secrecy. In lieu of reliable information, harmful office gossip and the grapevine spread rumors. Fear and apprehension replace trust, confidence, and loyalty. Consequently, a dictatorial office environment breeds and nurtures a corporate atmosphere receptive to violent behavior.

Employees believe that resistance and lashing out at authority are the only options available to overcome a sense of helpless subjugation. Former Provost Marshal for the Army's Training and Doctrine Command Colonel Richard Pomager Jr. stated, "You're a lot more likely to have incidents of violence if your workforce has the sense that anything goes and nobody cares."

Relaxation is a commodity that few can afford in today's rapid-paced society. The lack of rest and quality time caused by a highly competitive job environment builds stress, frustration, and eventually anger—anger that could result in violent acts aimed at supervision, another employee, customers, or property. Pagers and handheld mobile phones deny people the opportunity to unwind at the end of the day. The office, work, or deadlines are always just a phone call away.

States Dr. Martin Beahl, a psychiatrist at St. Bartholomew's Hospital, London, "Communication tools of modern life—fax machines, beepers, the mobile phone—are exacerbating these pressures. They are pernicious for mental health. In the old days when someone contacted you, you would think about it and then communicate in writing, but with the mobile phone they may require your response while driving or (while) sitting in the lavatory."

The automation age has contributed to job-related stress. Even though the workforce has been reduced, management expects (and demands) quality work to be expeditiously produced. Office automation has made it possible to generate reports and presentations in a matter of hours, as opposed to the days when someone typed reports and illustrators prepared charts and graphs. Ah, for the good old days, when there was no time for last-minute cosmetic changes. The endless stream of (re)work in a reduced-force environment adds to employee stress and frustration.

Employees bring "baggage" with them to the office. Often when a man is served with divorce papers or a restraining order, he stalks his wife at her place of work. In the majority of cases, men are the abusers and women the abused.

> . . . The stress associated with family problems feeds fuel to the highly combustible workplace environment. During times of emotional tensions, depressed individuals are likely to react violently.
>
> (Excerpted from John di Genio, "Office Rage—The Modern Craze," *Armed Forces Comptroller*, March 22, 2001.)

by being rejected; the employee may be feeling overlooked in not receiving a desired promotion; or the employee may be experiencing rage due to the knowledge of a potential layoff.

The Stressful Workplace

In their 2004 in-depth publication called *Overwork in America*, the Families and Work Institute found that one-third of all U.S. employees are chronically overworked. Downsizing, global competition, 24/7 operations, and dual careers have enhanced the products and services we are able to purchase as consumers. However, these same factors have increased the demands placed on us as producers—that is, in the workplace. And many of us, as individuals and as organizations, have not yet adjusted to this brave new world.

Many of us are working longer hours. But even more significant is the way we work today. Especially important is an increasing inability to focus on our work, because of constant interruptions and distractions and excessive multitasking (required to keep up with all that has to be done). Other factors identified in the Families and Work Institute's study include

- job pressure—not enough time to get everything done
- low-value work—spending time doing things perceived as a waste of time
- accessibility—contact with work outside normal work hours
- working while on vacation—or unused vacation

THE CONSEQUENCES

The more overworked employees are, the more likely they are to make mistakes at work, feel angry at their employers, and resent their coworkers. In addition to such work-related outcomes are the personal ones: higher levels of stress, poorer health, self-neglect, and increased symptoms of clinical depression.

In fact, the Families and Work Institute found that 26 percent of workers are often or very burned out or stressed by their work. And the St. Paul Fire and Marine Insurance Company determined that problems at work are more strongly associated with health complaints than are any other life stressor—more so than even financial or family problems.

THE MONETARY IMPACT

It has been estimated that as much as $300 billion (or $7,500 per employee) is spent annually in the United States on stress-related

- compensation claims, health insurance costs, and direct medical expenses
- reduced productivity, absenteeism, and employee turnover

This is not good news. This first decade of the new millennium is the era of working smarter and harder, 24/7. These very standards that demand high performance are having a negative impact on that performance—and on employee stress.

In Step 5, we will show you what the organization and individuals can do to keep the workplace from becoming a breeding ground for workplace violence and to minimize stress.

Detect

Behavioral Profiles

No one can predict human behavior with absolute certainty. However, indicators of increased risk of violent behavior are available. These indicators have been identified by the FBI's National Center for the Analysis of Violent Crime (NCAVC), Profiling and Behavioral Assessment Unit in its analysis of past incidents of workplace violence.

Formula for Workplace Violence

We created the acronym POSTAL to organize these indicators and other clues that are available to identify a potential workplace violence perpetrator, whether employee, personal relation, customer, or stranger. (Because of a few notorious incidents a couple of decades ago, the phrase "going postal" is often used when speaking about incidents of workplace violence. This phrase and our acronym in no way should be taken as deprecating those heroes who have died in the line of duty and all their coworkers who continue to risk their lives to deliver the mail—in the finest tradition of the U.S. Postal Service.)

By "profile," we mean behavioral characteristics (*not* racial profiling). In this case, we mean previous behavior. "Observable warning signs" also are behavioral, but now the focus is current behavior. "Shotgun" is access to and familiarity with any weapon (but we needed an S for the acronym). A "triggering event" is that last straw, or set of straws, which sets off the violence-prone individual. (Note: "Shotgun" is not required for nonlethal violence.)

Profile + **O**bservable warning signs + **S**hotgun + **T**riggering event(s) = **A**lways **L**ethal

---

Each of these elements is illustrated in the following classic case study (excerpted from Michael D. Kelleher in *New Arenas for Violence*) of the first person to "go postal." See if you can spot them.

"Going Postal"

In August 1986, 44-year-old postal employee Patrick Sherrill, dressed in his usual blue uniform and carrying a mailbag over his shoulder, walked into the U.S. Post Office in Edmond, OK. On this day, though, inside his mail pouch were two loaded .45-caliber pistols he had checked out from the National Guard Armory (where he was a member of the marksmanship team). He also carried over 300 rounds of ammunition and a .22-caliber handgun, which was his own property.

Sherrill said nothing as he immediately walked up to the shift supervisor and shot him in the chest. Still silent, Sherrill stalked more victims throughout the post office. His rampage lasted for only 10 minutes but during that time, he managed to murder 13 more employees (wounding 6 others). In a final act of violence, Sherrill turned one of the guns on himself and committed suicide.

This horrific crime inaugurated the era of the violent workplace in the press and the minds of many Americans. At the time, it was the third worst mass murder in American history.

Why did he do it? This was a man a onetime neighbor described as shy and gentle, who liked the words "thank you" and "please." Speculation ranged from post-traumatic stress syndrome to a poor performance review. A few employees said they thought Sherrill's murderous rampage was an act of revenge.

The morning before the murders, Sherrill had met with the shift supervisor and senior supervisor to discuss his work performance. It is believed that the senior supervisor threatened to terminate Sherrill. He was scheduled to meet with his supervisor the morning of the murders to discuss performance issues.

Sherrill had been a Marine sharpshooter and Vietnam War veteran. Before his job as letter carrier, he held a number of short-term jobs as file clerk, stockroom worker, and bicycle repairman. Throughout his life, Sherrill held a strong fascination for weapons and was highly proficient in their use. He was in a position to acquire weapons quickly and easily.

Patrick Sherrill had lived on the same street for twenty years. His neighbors referred to him as "Crazy Pat" because of his strange behavior in the neighborhood. He would, at times, mow his lawn at midnight, peer into neighbors' windows while wearing combat fatigues, or tie up neighborhood dogs with bailing wire. He was, by many neighborhood accounts, a loner and a strange individual. Sherrill had lived with his mother all his life until her death in 1974; after that he lived alone.

At work, people viewed Sherrill as often angry and frequently depressed. Coworkers perceived him as a problem employee. They said he preferred his own company to normal workplace socialization. Some described him as a habitual complainer and a consistent nonperformer. He was enigmatic and not well understood by anyone who knew him. This would later prove to be the common profile for a potentially violent employee.

Profile

Before we begin the behavioral profile, a brief word on the demographic profile. Notice that Patrick Sherrill was a forty-four-year-old man. Indeed, "middle-aged male" is the stereotype, and a somewhat accurate one. The vast majority of perpetrators of physical workplace violence (not necessarily verbal or electronic violence) are male, and many are middle-aged.

Our main reason for even commenting on the age aspect of the profile is that it is the opposite of the street crime profile. However, there are far too many exceptions for it to be useful. For example, Seung-Hui Cho of Virginia Tech was in his early twenties and Harris and Klebold of Columbine were still in their teens. (Note: The similarities between workplace violence and school violence are greater than the differences; and high schools and universities *are* work-places. Because of their notoriety, we include Cho, Harris, and Klebold among our examples illustrating the POSTAL elements.)

All workplace violence perpetrators previously displayed several of the following six behavioral characteristics.

1. PREVIOUS HISTORY OF VIOLENCE

Our first factor is the single most significant. This history of violence usually is toward those most vulnerable. For example, Patrick Sherrill tied up neighborhood dogs with bailing wire. Eric Harris of Columbine also tortured animals.

Other vulnerable prior victims are women or children. Mark Barton murdered his wife and children just before his day-trading massacre, and he was suspected by the police of having murdered his first wife. Wife beaters and child abusers are prime candidates for workplace violence.

This could also include violent artistic expression—for example, as in the two plays written by Virginia Tech's Cho and the video produced by Harris and Klebold of Columbine.

2. LONER

Typically, perpetrators are withdrawn and socially isolated. For example, Patrick Sherrill lived with his mother until her death, then lived alone during the last twelve years of his life. Harris and Klebold weren't even members of the anti-clique Trenchcoat Mafia, only on its fringes. And Cho certainly was a loner.

- A loner also feels nobody listens to him—no one is on his side.
- He views change with fear and suspicion and as a personal affront.

3. EMOTIONAL PROBLEMS

These may include any of the following:

- substance abuse or other self-destructive behavior—not an issue for Sherrill, but usually associated with nonlethal violence
- unresolved mental health problems (e.g., depression)— evidenced by Sherrill, Cho, and the boys of Columbine, and consistent with the lethal violence profile
- elevated frustration level and temper-control difficulties—also an issue for Sherrill
- low self-esteem—where one's sense of worth is tied to the job, a group, or a person (Remember this when we talk about obsessions and triggering events.)

4. CAREER FRUSTRATION

This often is reflected in either significant tenure on the same job or migratory job history. In Sherrill's case, it was migratory. Other examples of career frustration (to which we will refer again in triggering events) include Mark Barton's losses in the stock market and Eric Harris's rejection by the Air Force Academy.

5. ANTAGONISTIC RELATIONSHIP WITH OTHERS

Here are some of the traits of a person who is prone to violence:

- externalizes blame for life disappointments
- is disgruntled and has disdain for authority (e.g., Sherrill was a habitual complainer)
- threatens, intimidates, or harasses others (e.g., Cho's interaction with female students)
- has interpersonal problems and conflicts

6. OBSESSION

Our final profile attribute is the second most significant. In Sherrill's case, it certainly included obsession with weapons and other acts of violence. But it also could be:

- zealotry—whether political, religious, or racial (e.g., the Lockheed-Martin perpetrator and the 9/11 terrorists)
- a romantic or sexual obsession (e.g., Cho and his stalking incidents; see also the Romantic Stalker case study at the end of this chapter)
- the job itself (Keep this one in mind when we talk about triggering events.)
- even an extreme concern with neatness and order (See the Violent Security Guard case study at the end of this chapter.)

A WORD OF CAUTION

It is important to bear in mind, however, that having any one or even two of these characteristics does not mean someone will become violent. (A history of violence and some of the obsessions are exceptions.)

There are millions of people who are frustrated in their careers, who suffer from depression or anxiety, or who are introverts—who will never commit violence. It's the profile characteristics as a total picture that distinguishes the potential workplace violence perpetrator. As Dr. Lynn McClure observes in her book *Risky Business*: "In combination, they form patterns that signal lack of responsibility, lack of self-management, and lack of concern for others—patterns which, under intense situations, easily increase the potential for violence."

Applying the Profile

This is all very interesting, but how can you as a workplace leader use this information? You can be on the alert for attributes in the profile as you interact with coworkers, review personnel files, and especially, during the hiring process. Look for signs of the profile as you conduct

- critical reviews of information on resumés and applications
- in-depth interviews
- validated drug and psychological testing
- background checks—employment, criminal, credit, etc.

Are we saying that you should refuse to hire someone who, for example, has ever had a mental health problem (and thereby violate ADA or Rehabilitation Act regulations)? No, of course not. But if you also detect other factors, certainly proceed with caution and investigate further—for example, doing a more in-depth background check that includes neighbors and acquaintances. Notice in the "Going Postal" case study that some of Patrick Sherrill's behavior was observed only by his neighbors.

That's the profile. For your existing workforce—and when dealing with outsiders—we turn to the next important topic.

Observable Warning Signs

These warning signs, which can be newly acquired negative traits, parallel and overlap the profile, but now we focus on current behavior.

1. VIOLENT AND THREATENING BEHAVIOR

For Patrick Sherrill, it was tying up neighborhood dogs with bailing wire and a strong fascination for weapons. In general, this also includes

- destruction of property or threats of sabotage
- disregard for the safety of others or violation of safety procedures
- threats, intimidation, bullying—for example, Cho and the boys of Columbine (as both perpetrators and victims)
- violence against a family member—for example, Mark Barton
- stalking or harassing others (Cho was involved in at least three stalking incidents, the first occurring eighteen months prior to his rampage. Also, he placed harassing phone calls to his roommate and took cell phone pictures of female students' legs under their desks.)

2. STRANGE BEHAVIOR

Patrick Sherrill's neighbors noted his strange behavior in the neighborhood—mowing his lawn at midnight and peering into neighbors' windows while wearing combat fatigues. His coworkers said he preferred his own company and described him as enigmatic. Cho was known as "the question-mark kid." He had an imaginary girlfriend who lived in outer space.

In general, strange behavior can include

- becoming reclusive—that is, a sudden withdrawal from friends or acquaintances (Mark Barton's means of earning a living became increasingly isolating.)
- poor personal hygiene or a deteriorating and unkempt appearance
- inappropriate dress; for example, Cho never took off his sunglasses, even indoors
- bizarre or paranoid behavior
- erratic behavior or an extreme change in behavior

3. EMOTIONAL PROBLEMS

For example, Patrick Sherrill was often angry and frequently depressed. A district court found Cho to be "an imminent danger to himself as a result of mental illness." Professors described him as insecure and depressed, as were the boys of Columbine. This also can include

- drug or alcohol abuse
- appearing to be under unusual stress; signs of depression or despondence
- inappropriate emotional display—for example, screaming, explosive outbursts, rage, crying

4. PERFORMANCE PROBLEMS

Sherrill's coworkers perceived him as a problem employee and a consistent nonperformer. Virginia Tech declined to divulge details about Cho's academic record, but Cho's mother was increasingly concerned about his inattention to classwork and his time spent out of the classroom. Performance problems also can include

- inability to concentrate; decreased energy or focus
- deteriorating work performance
- attendance or tardiness problems
- increased need for supervision (Coworkers have to take up the slack.)

5. INTERPERSONAL PROBLEMS

Cho was described as awkward and lonely; arrogant and obnoxious; timid, dorky, and pushy. Sherrill was a habitual complainer. This also can include

- numerous conflicts with supervisors and other employees
- hypersensitivity or extreme suspiciousness
- resentment and frustration
- exaggerated perceptions of injustice

6. AT THE END OF HIS ROPE

The last warning sign on our list is also the last warning sign a potential perpetrator probably will display. For example:

- has a plan to solve all problems (What do you think that plan might entail?)
- indicators of impending suicide (e.g., selling property, closing credit union account)

- other indications of extreme desperation, marital discord, financial distress, etc.

Cho purchased guns in the two months preceding his rampage, spent time at a local target range, began working out at the gym, and shaved his head military style. Also, there was the media package Cho sent to NBC News. (It was not received until after the massacre, of course, but wouldn't his roommates have had some awareness of its preparation?)

Shotgun

"Shotgun" simply is access to and familiarity with weapons—not only shotguns, but also handguns, rifles, explosives, and knives or box cutters—and also martial arts training. Patrick Sherrill certainly had such access and familiarity, and Cho and the boys of Columbine acquired it.

Shotgun is not a warning sign. Hunters and gun collectors are not more likely to commit workplace violence, unless they're obsessed with their guns. It's just that, without access to and familiarity with weapons, that violence probably won't be lethal.

Triggering Event(s)

The triggering event is the last straw or set of straws—experienced by the perpetrator as no way out, no more options. This could be . . .

1. JOB/CAREER RELATED

Patrick Sherrill's rampage appeared to be an act of revenge for a poor performance review. The morning before the murders, the senior supervisor threatened to terminate Sherrill, and he was scheduled to meet with his immediate supervisor the morning of the murders to discuss performance issues. Remember the significance of obsession with the job in the profile. Other examples include Mark Barton's losses in the stock market and Eric Harris of Columbine, who had just been rejected by the Air Force Academy.

But job/career-related events—such as being disciplined or fired or even criticized—are only one type of triggering event. It can also be . . .

2. INSTITUTIONAL

The triggering event could be related to foreclosure on a mortgage, bankruptcy, a restraining order, or a custody hearing. For example, in 1995, a forty-seven-year-old man shot and killed his pregnant wife and two of her friends who were waiting to testify at his annulment hearing outside a Seattle courtroom. (See also the "Romantic Stalker" case study at the end of this chapter for an example of a restraining order as a triggering event.)

3. PERSONAL CRISIS

This can be, for example, a divorce, a death in the family, or a failed or spurned romance—as it may have been for Eric Harris, whose girlfriend had recently broken up with him. Also in Littleton, Colorado, four years earlier, a thirty-five-year-old man, distraught over marital problems, opened fire in a crowded grocery store, killing three people (including his wife) before being subdued.

It may even be a . . .

4. BENCHMARK DATE

This could be, for example, turning forty, or a ten-year company anniversary . . . and feeling he's going nowhere in life. Or the anniversary of some other event that is significant to the individual.

The Columbine massacre occurred on April 20. Do you know whose birthday that is? Adolf Hitler's. Not a date most of us celebrate or even know, but significant to these two budding neo-Nazis.

All of us have experienced an unpleasant event in our life, which probably triggered negative feelings. Such events can trigger violence in those already primed for it—those who fit the profile and/or display the observable warning signs. These events would tend to shake anyone's sense of balance, at least temporarily. A violence-prone person already is unbalanced. The triggering event pushes him over the edge.

Applying the Warning Signs and Triggering Events

Look for the observable warning signs and triggering events as you

- deal with your employees on a day-to-day basis
- interact with customers—and observe strangers

How you handle individuals who exhibit the warning signs will vary considerably depending on the severity and situation. At a minimum, sit down and listen to the troubled employee or customer.

THE ONE ABSOLUTE: NEVER IGNORE!

In the words of the husband of one of the victims at Lockheed Martin: "Obviously, he was a sick guy. I wish somebody had given him some help—before he destroyed my life and my kids' life."

Level 1: Confusion
• Bewilderment or distraction • Unsure of next course of action

Level 2: Frustration
• Strong reaction or resistance to information • Impatience • A sense of defeat in the attempt of accomplishment;   attempts to bait you

Level 3: Blame
• Placing responsibility for problems on everyone else • Accusing or holding you responsible • Finding fault or error with the actions of others • May place blame directly on you • Crossing over to potentially hazardous behavior

Level 4: Anger
• Changes in body posture and disposition • Physical actions like pounding fists, pointing fingers,   shouting, and screaming

Level 5: Hostility
• Physical actions or threats that appear imminent • Acts of physical harm or property damage • Out-of-control behaviors that signal they have crossed the   line

Figure 2.1.   Five levels of instability.

Five Levels of Instability

The following levels of instability are summarized in figure 2.1 and can be useful in assessing the severity of an individual's behavior, whether an employee, customer, or stranger:

Level 1: Confusion
Level 2: Frustration

Level 3: Blame
Level 4: Anger
Level 5: Hostility

PREVENTING EMPLOYEE VIOLENCE

If an employee begins demonstrating any or a combination of the above indicators (short of Level 5: hostility, physical violence, or threats), it is important that management refer him or her to the Employee Assistance Program (EAP) or other counseling services as soon as possible. It is imperative to respond in an empathic, caring, and nonshaming manner, remembering that time is of the essence.

Our prescription for preventing employee-initiated violence is

- benevolent, motivational management practices (Some organizations are breeding grounds for violence.)
- appropriate use of counseling, EAP, disciplinary action, and/or law enforcement
- employee and management training (All employees need to know about the warning signs, and the anger-defusing techniques covered in the next step.)
- sound security measures, which, at a minimum, eliminate "shotgun" from the equation
- a zero-tolerance violence policy—effectively communicated and enforced (A clarification about zero tolerance: This term is often used to mean applying the same severe punishment for even minor offenses. That is not what we mean. Minor offenses and potential red flags should never be tolerated or ignored, but your response should be proportional and appropriate.)

These all will be explored in much greater depth in the remaining steps.

Oftentimes, violence in the workplace is committed by someone from outside the business. Therefore, when possible, it is important to have surveillance at the entrance of the workplace. The following visitors represent a potential danger:

- the spouse or partner of an employee who is in an abusive relationship
- rejected suitors; partners involved in divorce or separation procedures
- ex-employees who have been fired or laid off
- disgruntled customers
- person committing armed robbery
- persons involved in gang activities
- in school settings, parents who feel their child has been treated unfairly or students who have been suspended

Violence by Strangers

Preventive strategies for Type 1 violence (by strangers) include an emphasis on physical security measures, special employer policies, and employee training. In fact, it is suggested that one of the reasons for the decline in workplace homicides since the early 1990s is due to the security measures put in place by businesses that may be vulnerable to this type of activity.

Because the outside criminal has no other contact with the workplace, the interpersonal aspects of violence prevention that apply to the other three categories are normally not relevant to Type 1 incidents. The response after a crime has occurred will involve conventional law enforcement procedures for investigating, finding, and arresting the suspect, and collecting evidence for prosecution. For that reason, even though Type 1 events represent a large share of workplace violence (homicides in particular) and should in no way be minimized, this (book) focuses primarily on the remaining types. . . .

(Type 3 and Type 4 violence) is no less or more dangerous or damaging than any other violent act. But when the violence comes from an employee or someone close to an employee, there is a much greater chance that some warning sign will have reached the employer in the form of observable behavior. That knowledge, along with the appropriate prevention programs, can at the very least mitigate the potential for violence or prevent it altogether.

(Excerpted from the FBI's *Workplace Violence: Issues in Response*.)

Detecting Domestic Violence

According to the American Bar Association Commission on Domestic Violence, "domestic violence is a pattern of behavior in which one intimate partner uses physical violence, coercion, threats, intimidation, isolation, and emotional, sexual, or economic abuse to control the other partner in a relationship. Stalking or other harassing behavior is often an integral part of domestic violence." (See *A Guide for Employees: Domestic Violence in the Workplace*, quoted in the FBI's *Workplace Violence*.)

In the same guide, the American Bar Association's Commission on Domestic Violence says that the following observable behavior may suggest possible victimization (quoted in the FBI's *Workplace Violence*):

- tardiness or unexplained absences
- frequent—and often unplanned—use of leave time
- anxiety
- lack of concentration
- change in job performance
- a tendency to remain isolated from coworkers or reluctance to participate in social events

- discomfort when communicating with others
- disruptive phone calls or e-mail
- sudden or unexplained requests to be moved from public locations in the workplace, such as sales or reception areas
- frequent financial problems, indicating lack of access to money
- unexplained bruises or injuries
- noticeable change in use of makeup (to cover up injuries)
- inappropriate clothes (e.g., sunglasses worn inside the building, turtleneck worn in the summer)
- disruptive visits from current or former intimate partner
- sudden changes of address or reluctance to divulge where the employee is staying
- acting uncharacteristically moody, depressed, or distracted
- in the process of ending an intimate relationship; breakup seems to cause the employee undue anxiety
- court appearances
- being the victim of vandalism or threats

Detecting Terrorism

Terrorist attacks are seldom spontaneous and usually involve weeks of careful planning and preparation. Planning includes surveillance of the target—perhaps your building. If you see people parked for long periods near your building and maybe taking notes or photographs, report it to the authorities. If strangers strike up a conversation and ask sensitive questions about your workplace, report it. If you see anything suspicious, never take action yourself. Take notes and report it—it is always better to be safe than sorry.

The following information comes from the National Terror Alert Response Center (www.nationalterroralert.com/suspicious-activity):

When taking notes, be sure to SALUTE—that is, include each of the following:

Size (Jot down the number of people, gender, ages, and physical descriptions.)
Activity (Describe exactly what they are doing.)
Location (Provide exact location.)
Uniform (Describe what they are wearing, including shoes.)
Time (Provide date, time, and duration of activity.)
Equipment (Describe vehicle, make, color, etc., license plate, camera, guns, etc.)

Suspicious activity is often recalled after an event. We must train ourselves to be on the lookout for things that are out of the ordinary and arouse suspicion—*before* the event.

Keep in mind that those who commit terrorist acts

- usually live among us without appearing suspicious while planning and preparing for their attack; they may be your neighbors, students, or friends
- often will need training or equipment that will arouse suspicion
- need to conduct surveillance on possible targets and gather information on the planned attack location

All of these things make terrorists vulnerable to detection by those watching for certain characteristics. Learn to recognize the difference between normal and abnormal behavior. It can be a fine line. Stay alert in your daily travels and routines and get to know

- who your neighbors are
- what cars are normally in your neighborhood
- who regularly makes deliveries at work and in your neighborhood

Staying alert is *not* about becoming paranoid. Staying alert is being aware of one's surroundings. Be alert to indications of possible trouble. They may include

- a local activity that could indicate problems in your community
- commemoration of violent acts (One of the clues that led to the recent breakup of a terrorist plot was that several of the cell members were spotted celebrating in an apartment complex on the anniversary of 9/11.)
- previous activity or crimes
- controversial issues being debated
- suspicious thefts

It is impossible to identify a terrorist by

- appearance
- nationality
- language

You can only identify a terrorist threat by observing or hearing about suspicious activity that may lead to a criminal act.

Identifying suspicious activity is not a difficult science. Rely on your judgment. Your suspicion of a threat could be confirmed with only one incident, or it could take a series of incidents. Your suspicions will need to be based on

- experience
- judgment
- common sense

REVIEW POSSIBLE SUSPICIOUS ACTIVITY

Here is just one example.

Unusual Interest in High Risk or Symbolic Targets

Maybe you are at a high-profile location, or perhaps a national monument, and you notice a person nearby taking several photos. That's not unusual. But then you notice that the person is only taking photos of the locations of surveillance cameras, entrance crash barriers, and access control procedures. Is that normal for a tourist? No.

The following should cause a heightened sense of suspicion:

- suspicious or unusual interest
- surveillance (suspicious in nature)
- inappropriate photographs or videos
- note-taking
- drawing of diagrams
- annotating maps
- using binoculars or night vision devices

Unusual or suspicious activity does not necessarily mean that terrorist activity is happening, but be aware of the following suspicious behaviors:

- individuals acting furtively and suspiciously
- individuals avoiding eye contact
- individuals departing quickly when seen or approached
- individuals in places they don't belong
- a strong odor coming from a building or vehicle
- an overloaded vehicle
- fluid leaking from a vehicle, other than the engine or gas tank
- individuals overdressed for the type of weather

FRAUDULENT IDENTIFICATION

Many of the 9/11 terrorists were in the country illegally and using fraudulent IDs. Altering or using false government identification in any way and for any purpose is against the law.

Fraudulent IDs include

- driver's license
- Social Security card
- passport

- birth certificate
- INS identification

If you believe someone is using or has altered government identification, notify the law enforcement authorities. Do *not* request to see another person's ID when not appropriate. Allow law enforcements to do the investigating.

Terrorists, when not acting alone, need to meet with their conspirators and often work within a cell. Pay attention to visitors and guests that

- arrive and leave at unusual hours
- try not to be noticed
- act in a suspicious manner
- park an unusual distance from the meeting
- have an unusual number of unrelated people living together

Not all people who maintain privacy are terrorists. But people intent on doing illegal acts want to be left alone.

Some signs that may raise your suspicions:

- They only let you into the apartment or house with plenty of prior notice.
- They change the locks often.
- They keep certain rooms off limits.
- They cover tables and other pieces of furniture.
- They never allow maid service in a hotel room.
- They only take hotel room service outside the door.
- They only accept deliveries at the hotel's front desk or outside a closed door.

Deliveries are a common method for terrorists to carry out their attacks. Be aware of

- a vehicle with hazardous material parked or driving in an inappropriate area
- unusual deliveries of chemicals or fertilizer
- unattended bags or boxes in a public access place
- fire extinguishers that may have been moved or tampered with
- unusual or unexpected mail

UNUSUAL PURCHASES OR THEFTS

Terrorists need supplies to carry out their attacks and accomplish their goals. Pay attention to purchases, rentals, or thefts of

- police, security, public utility, mail carrier, or airline uniforms and equipment
- explosives
- weapons
- ammunition
- propane bottles
- toxic chemicals
- vehicles able to contain or haul hazardous materials

Additional suspicious activity may include

- someone bragging or talking about plans to harm citizens in violent attacks or who claims membership in a terrorist organization that espouses killing innocent people
- suspicious packages, luggage, or mail that have been abandoned in a crowded place like an office building, an airport, a school, or a shopping center
- suspicious letter or package that arrives in your mailbox (Stay away from the letter or package and don't shake, bump, or sniff it; wash hands thoroughly with soap and water.)
- someone suspiciously exiting a secured, nonpublic area near a train or bus depot, airport, tunnel, bridge, government building, or tourist attraction
- any type of activity or circumstance that seems frightening or unusual within the normal routines of your neighborhood, community, and workplace
- someone unfamiliar loitering in a parking lot, government building, or around a school or playground
- anyone asking a lot of questions, especially concerning routes or loads or drop-off times
- Recruiters should be alert for unusual employment applications. Don't assume it couldn't be an inside job.
- A trucker returning to his or her vehicle from a restaurant or truck stop should make sure no one is loitering around the truck. Watch out for walk-arounds.

Workplace Violence Case Studies

For each of the following real-life case studies, apply the Formula for Workplace Violence—that is:

1. In what way did the perpetrator fit the profile?
2. What observable warning signs did he exhibit?
3. What access to and familiarity with weapons (shotgun) did he have?

4. What was the triggering event?

5. What could have been done to prevent the incident?

CASE STUDY 1: THE ROMANTIC STALKER

After a ten-year stint in the Navy, software technician Richard Farley, thirty-six, joined Electromagnetic Systems Labs in 1984. There he met Laura Black, a twenty-two-year-old electrical engineer. During court testimony, Farley said, "I think I fell instantly in love with her." For the next three and a half years, Farley deluged her with two hundred letters, telephoned her at any hour, left gifts on her desk, and rifled through her personnel files. He trailed her everywhere—to and from work, driving past her home at night, even joining her aerobics class. He twice tried to move into her apartment building. Farley often asked her for a date, but was always turned aside politely by Laura. Rejections would inevitably bring on recurring protestations and endless restatements of his limitless love for her. Laura did what she could to avoid him and deter his advances. She was forced to move twice.

Eventually, Farley could no longer take no for an answer, and his tactics became aggressive and cruel. He made derogatory statements about her, and each contact became increasingly offensive.

When Laura finally complained to her employer in the fall of 1985, they instructed Farley to stop and to seek psychological help. Though he did attend counseling sessions, the harassment did not diminish—it elevated. He made a duplicate copy of Laura's house key, displaying it and a note on the dashboard of his car so she would know he could get to her at any time. His letters became more threatening, sometimes referring to his large gun collection. In 1986, he publicly and vehemently threatened her life. He also began threatening other employees, including a manager, whom he warned about his gun collection, his expertise with guns, and the fact that he "could take people with him" if provoked.

ESL fired Farley in May 1986. Just before that, he wrote to Laura, "Once I'm fired, you won't be able to control me . . . I'll crack under . . . and run amok and destroy everything in my path." For the next one and a half years, he continued to harass her. He wrote in November 1987, "You cost me a job, 40 thousand in equity taxes and a foreclosure. Yet I still like you. Why do you want to find out how far I'll go?"

On February 8, 1988, Laura got a temporary restraining order against him, with a hearing scheduled for February 17. On February 9, Farley purchased a 12-gauge semiautomatic shotgun and ammunition.

On February 16 (two days after Valentine's Day and the day before the final hearing), Farley approached his ex-employer's building, wearing one hundred pounds of weaponry (including his new shotgun, a rifle, two handguns, bandoliers of ammunition, and a container of gasoline). Farley killed his first victim in the parking lot. At the entrance, he blasted his way through the locked glass doors. En route to Laura's office, Farley fired indiscriminately at anyone in his path, killing four more and wounding another four. Laura had locked herself in her office—to no avail. Farley blew her office door off its hinges with his shotgun. He shot Laura twice. Although seriously injured, she survived. Farley's siege lasted five hours with a SWAT team. At the end, seven employees were dead and four wounded. When apprehended, Farley expressed no shame but seemed almost gleeful. He was convicted of seven counts of murder and four felonies, and received the death sentence in 1992.

At the time of his rampage, Richard Farley was thirty-nine years old. The oldest of six children of an Air Force mechanic and his wife, whose household moved frequently. Richard was an isolated child. His classmates considered him a "wimp," and he had no close friends. Those who knew him in the Navy found him to be a loner, egotistical and arrogant. When he worked at ESL, Farley was a pudgy, bespectacled man with a puffy face. He was a collector of weapons, power tools, and numerous books dealing with sex and violence. He had no prior criminal record whatsoever. (For more details, see Michael Kelleher, *Profiling the Lethal Employee*.)

CASE STUDY 2: THE VIOLENT SECURITY GUARD

"Spacey Sam," a thirty-four-year-old white male, was a contract security guard who worked for eighteen months at a mental health/drug rehab agency in the Southeast.

On March 10, 2004, he was terminated for poor performance. An administrative assistant was assigned the task of terminating him. She told him that he was being fired and had to pack up and leave the building immediately. She then, unescorted, led him into a stairwell so they could go to the second floor to get his things. It was at this time that he began yelling and punching her. She began fighting back, which only incited his rage. Fortunately, the altercation was overheard, and a male coworker, shortly followed by others, entered the stairwell and pulled Sam off her. Sam was then arrested.

During a March 8 meeting to discuss his performance problems, "he didn't make eye contact and he made weird faces" and "his stomach was growling." After that meeting, Sam began using more profanity. On March 9, he said to a detox counselor: "You guys better watch out; tomorrow there's going to be a smackdown." That evening, Sam said to the receptionist and to a contract cleaning person: "There are a lot of haters in this building."

Post-incident comments employees made about Spacey Sam:

- strange / spooky / weird / weird smile, weird affect / not all there
- missed social cues / didn't pick up on signals to end a conversation

- always asked people for money / borrowed money from support staff / from customers
- would stop and stand at people's door as if wanting to talk, but then not say anything
- tiptoed into an employee's office / snuck up behind people
- when you spoke to him, it looked like he wasn't looking at you, but staring through you
- not that bright / not very deep / had the mind of a child / high-functioning mentally retarded
- not your typical male / silly and passive / had no driver's license
- didn't always know where he was going once he started a conversation
- overly friendly (especially with women) / very friendly (though he became cooler over time)
- was formal and excessively polite / flattering
- had no friends here / though age 34, he lived with his father / had no girl-friends
- took a lot of breaks / frequently on the pay phone / often in lounge / attendance problems
- kinda did his job / harmless (to the point of being ineffective in a crisis) / a nuisance
- a customer observed that Sam carefully arranged the pencils on his desk, all with the points facing the same way, and became upset when she didn't put the cap back on a pen she had borrowed from him.
- loved being a security guard / taken with his uniform (inflated sense of power and importance)
- acted as if he worked in a jail / miscommunicated an Anthrax drill, frightening employees
- had a hurt look on his face whenever on-site supervisor gave him feedback
- got upset when teased by female front desk staff—came running to on-site supervisor

CASE STUDY 3—DOMESTIC VIOLENCE

On the evening of November 8, 2001, Ana Melina Kilic was at her job in a hair-accessory shop in Harborplace, Baltimore's showpiece downtown tourist and shopping area. At about 7 p.m., her ex-husband, Imamali Kilic, appeared in the shop with a butcher knife.

Ana Kilic fled screaming into the corridor. Imamali Kilic overtook her, grabbed her, and according to more than twenty horrified witnesses, stabbed her again and again. He kept stabbing even when about a dozen onlookers, one of them wielding a baseball bat from a nearby sports store, rushed to Ana Kilic's rescue. They eventually subdued him, but not in time to save his victim's life. An autopsy later determined that the twenty-eight-year-old Ana Kilic had been stabbed or slashed twenty-nine separate times. Imamali Kilic was arrested at the scene and charged with murder. Not quite four months later, he hanged himself in his cell at the Baltimore City Jail, where he was awaiting trial. After surviving for a few days on a respirator, he died on March 1, 2002.

The killing of Ana Kilic did not come unexpectedly out of the blue or without any efforts to prevent it. Quite the opposite. In August 2001, a day after an earlier confrontation in her shop, she went to court to ask for a restraining order against her husband, whose own workplace was in the same Harborplace pavilion, one floor below. Her petition alleged that he had raped her on two occasions and, in their encounter the previous day, had threatened her with violence. The court granted a week-long restraining order, but then dismissed the case when Ana Kilic did not come back to ask for its extension. About that time, the couple's divorce became final.

A little more than a month later, Ana Kilic complained to Baltimore police that her ex-husband had abducted her, taken her to New Jersey, and raped her again. Subsequently, according to police and court records, he made threatening calls to her home, warning that he would kill her and "cut off her arms and legs." He came to the shop and repeated the threats to her face, Ana Kilic told police. Arrested on charges of harassment and telephone misuse, Imamali Kilic spent a month in jail awaiting trial, then pleaded guilty to both offenses. Judge Paul A. Smith of the Baltimore Circuit Court sentenced him to three years of probation. The judge also ordered him to attend a program at a battered women's shelter and to have no contact with his ex-wife.

With that, Imamali Kilic was released from jail. One day later, Ana Kilic was murdered. (Excerpted from the FBI's 2004 report on *Workplace Violence*.)

CASE STUDY 4—TERRORISM

The Oklahoma City Bombing on April 18, 1995, was a domestic terrorist attack aimed at the U.S. government and federal workers. The attack on the Alfred P. Murrah Federal Building in downtown Oklahoma City claimed 168 lives and injured over 800. It remains the deadliest act of domestic terrorism on U.S. soil.

A rented Ryder truck was packed with 108 fifty-pound bags of ammonium nitrate fertilizer, three fifty-five-gallon drums of liquid nitromethane, several crates of the explosive Tovex, seventeen bags of ANFO (the most widely used explosive in mining), and spools of shock tube and cannon fuse that had been mixed together. It was then parked in a drop-off zone under the building's day care center.

The attack was carried out by twenty-six-year-old Timothy McVeigh with the help of Terry Nichols. Both were sympathizers of a militia group and the attack was carried out to protest the government's handling of the Waco and Ruby Ridge incidents—the bombing occurred on the second anniversary of the Waco incident. As he drove to the federal building McVeigh was wearing a T-shirt with the motto of the Commonwealth of Virginia—"Thus Ever to Tyrants"—which was shouted by John Wilkes Booth after he assassinated Abraham Lincoln. McVeigh also carried an envelope containing pages from *The Turner Diaries*, a fictional account of modern-day revolutionaries who rise up against the government and incite a race war.

McVeigh's hatred of the government started while he was serving in the army. After his discharge he became a drifter, spending some time on the gun show circuit selling copies of *The Turner Diaries*. He became more convinced that the government was trampling on civil liberties and believed that militant action was the only answer. He told several people of his plans to blow up the Federal Building—but no one reported this to the authorities.

McVeigh was executed by lethal injection on June 11, 2001; Nichols was sentenced to life imprisonment.

Defuse and Protect

Our focus is now on how to protect yourself and your workplace from actual or potential violent incidents. This step includes the following:

- defusing hostile, potentially violent employees and customers
- protecting yourself and others when threatened with actual violence
- dealing with telephone threats
- self-protection tips
- domestic violence procedures
- ensuring physical security
- hiring security professionals
- law enforcement
- "What would you do if" scenarios

Defusing a Hostile Coworker or Customer

The POSTAL formula and its applications are intended to prevent violence in advance. But what can you do when confronted with a hostile, potentially violent employee or outsider? Well, we have an acronym for that as well.

Let's see if you can guess it. In a sense, POSTAL has become our metaphor for the potential workplace violence perpetrator. Well, what is the postal carrier's traditional nemesis? That's right: DOGS. By which we mean: Defusing Of Grievance = Safety.

Visualize a big balloon that's about to explode. Instead of puncturing the balloon with confrontation, you want to *gradually* deflate the balloon. You do this by confirming a person's perspective, without necessarily agreeing with it.

We learned the following six-point guideline from hostage negotiator Larry Chavez, of Critical Incident Associates (see www.workplace-violence.com):

1. **Understand the mindset of the hostile person.** He has a compelling need to communicate his grievance. Even if he's wrong, his perceptions are real to him. Usually the person just wants fairness. On the other hand, he probably is not reasonable, at least initially. Don't expect calm rationality or attempt to engage in problem solving too early in the process. A person in crisis will only respond favorably to someone who is believed to be understanding, willing to listen, worthy of respect, and nonthreatening. Most important— preserve the individual's dignity! Never belittle, embarrass or verbally attack a hostile person (or any person).

2. **Avoid confrontation.** Instead, have as your goal building trust and providing help. Remain calm and create a relaxed environment. Make sure you are courteous and respectful, patient and reasonable, open and honest. Avoid (a) challenging body language (e.g., crossed arms, pointing fingers, jaw thrust forward); (b) getting "in his face" (Respect personal space—at least three feet away.); (c) anger words (e.g., profanity, insults, etc.), over-familiarity, or extreme formality; and (d) hostile paraverbals (how you say what you say— your tone, volume and speed).

3. **Allow total airing of grievance without comment.** Permit verbal venting or ranting, but set and enforce reasonable limits. Be empathetic—tune in to the person's feelings, without judging. Make eye contact, but don't stare. And ignore challenges and insults. Don't take it personally; redirect attention to the real issue.

4. **Practice active listening.** Stop what you are doing and give the person your full attention. Use silence; don't rush in to attempt to complete his thoughts. Collect the facts on the problem: who, what, and when (leave why for later). Then go deeper—listen to what is really being said. What does the person want you to understand? Use reflective questioning to confirm that you've really heard: "Let me see if I understand you. Are you saying . . . ?" "You want . . . . Is that right?" And ask clarifying and open-ended questions to assist the person in getting it all off his or her chest: "Give me an example." "What would you like to see happen?" "Anything else?" "Tell me more."

5. **Allow the aggrieved party to suggest a solution.** Thus far, your primary goal has been to de-escalate the immediate situation. Now that the person has calmed down, he or she probably will be more open to a rational discussion of the issues. You're now ready to begin problem solving. Use inquiry to define the problem and to solicit the person's suggestions. Inquiry really is very simple, although not necessarily easy. You merely ask: "What do you think?" in a nonjudgmental way. By tone of voice and reputation, the

other person needs to be assured that whatever ideas or opinions he or she expresses will be OK. If necessary, get the person to open up by probing his or her prior experiences and perspectives. The person will more readily agree to what happens next, if he or she helped formulate it. And you may be surprised by how reasonable the person's suggestions now are. So what do you do if the person's ideas are not workable? Look for parts of the idea to build on or, at a minimum, credit the person for the idea and explain why you can't use it. Assure the person you'll act on any injustices he or she has suffered—and carry out your commitments.

6. **Move toward a win-win resolution.** Offer something and have the person do likewise. For example, offer to take specific actions to redress his or her grievance and request that the person refrain from future outbursts. With the person's permission, call in additional resources—for example, your boss, his or her boss, an HR representative, your Employee Assistance Program, even a security guard or the police, if warranted. (Yes, the person may very well agree to this. Now that he or she is calmed and has regained his or her reason, the person may realize that his or her actions have violated your policy or the law, and his or her own sense of honor.)

All of these suggestions for personal conduct are summarized in figure 3.1.

Suggestions for Responding to the Five Levels of Instability

In Step 2, we outlined five levels of instability. The following levels correspond to the suggested responses in figure 3.2 and can help you adapt the foregoing general guidelines to specific situations:

Level 1: Confusion
Level 2: Frustration
Level 3: Blame
Level 4: Anger
Level 5: Hostility

Defusing Practice Activity

Here is a good practice activity to help you become comfortable defusing hostile situations. There are four basic stages:

1. *Enlist* the services of someone with whom you feel comfortable to play an angry or upset person for this practice activity.

DO . . .	DO NOT . . .
• Project calmness. Move and speak slowly, quietly, and confidently.	• Use styles of communication that generate hostility, such as apathy, the brush-off, coldness, condescension, robotism, going strictly by the rules, or giving the run-around.
• Maintain a relaxed yet attentive posture, and position yourself at a right angle instead of directly in front of the other person.	
	• Reject the person's demands from the start.
• Arrange yourself so that the person cannot block access to your exit.	
	• Pose in challenging stances such as standing directly opposite someone, crossing your arms, or putting your hands on your hips.
• Be an empathetic listener. Encourage the person to talk, and listen patiently.	
• Focus your attention on the other person to let the person know that you are interested in what he or she has to say.	• Invade the person's personal space. Make sure there is a space of three to six feet between you.
• Acknowledge the person's feelings. Indicate that you understand that he or she is upset.	• Engage in any physical contact, finger pointing, or prolonged period of fixed eye contact.
• Ask for small, specific favors, such as asking to move to a quieter area.	• Make sudden movements that could be perceived as threatening.
• Establish ground rules if unreasonable behavior persists. Calmly describe the consequences of any violent behavior.	• Raise the tone, volume, or rate of your speech.
• Use delaying tactics that will give the person time to calm down. For example, offer a drink of water (in a disposable cup).	• Challenge, threaten, or dare the individual.
	• Belittle the person, or make him or her feel foolish.
• Be reassuring, and point out choices. Break big problems down into smaller, more manageable ones.	• Criticize or act impatiently.
	• Attempt to bargain.
• Accept criticism in a positive way. When a complaint might be true, use statements like "You are probably right" or "It was my fault." If the criticism seems unwarranted, ask clarifying questions.	• Try to make the situation seem less serious than it is.
	• Make false statements or promises you cannot keep.
	• Try to impart a lot of technical or complicated information when emotions are high.
• Ask for recommendations from the person. Repeat back what you feel he or she is requesting of you.	• Take sides or agree with distortions.

Figure 3.1. Suggestions for personal conduct.

LEVEL OF INSTABILITY	SUGGESTED RESPONSES
Level 1: Confusion	
• Bewilderment or distraction • Unsure of next course of action	• Listen to the person's concerns • Ask clarifying questions • Give the person factual information
Level 2: Frustration	
• Strong reaction or resistance to information • Impatience • A sense of defeat in the attempt of accomplishment; attempts to bait	• Relocate to a quiet setting • Reassure the person • Make a sincere attempt to clarify concerns
Level 3: Blame	
• Placing responsibility or finding fault with others • Accusing or holding you responsible • Crossing over to potentially hazardous behavior	• Disengage and bring third party into the discussion • Use teamwork approach • Draw the person back to the facts • Use probing questions • Create "yes" momentum
Level 4: Anger	
• Changes in body posture and disposition • Physical actions like pounding fists, pointing fingers, shouting, and screaming	• Use venting techniques • Don't offer solutions • Don't argue with comments made • Prepare to evacuate or isolate • Contact supervisor and/or security
Level 5: Hostility	
• Physical actions or threats that appear imminent • Acts of physical harm or property damage • Out-of-control behaviors that signal the person has crossed the line	• Attempt to isolate the person if it can be done safely • Disengage and evacuate • Alert supervisor and/or security immediately

Figure 3.2.   Responses to the five levels of instability.

2. Have that person *choose* one of the following situations or remember a time when he or she was upset, explain the situation to you, then *act* it out.

3. *Apply* the defusing guidelines and attempt to talk the person down. Better yet, listen the person down. Take whatever time is needed.

4. *Reflect* on what happened. Ask for feedback from your partner. What worked? For example, what did you say or do which tended to calm your partner and gain his or her trust? What didn't work as well? For example, what did you say or do that may have aggravated the situation or caused a stalemate at any point?

SITUATION 1: THE DEMANDING SUPERVISOR

Your supervisor has been making unrealistic demands (e.g., absurd deadlines) and has been verbally abusive when these demands are not met. You've had it up to here! Nothing you do is right.

SITUATION 2: THE DENIED INSURANCE CLAIM

Your health insurance provider has denied your medical insurance claim. It was for a somewhat unusual procedure to treat a serious condition of your child/spouse/self (select whatever is applicable to you). You—and your doctor—regard the procedure as absolutely necessary. You are furious.

SITUATION 3: THE WORK/FAMILY CRISIS

Occasionally, you need to take time off, come in late, or leave a bit early in order to take care of personal business (e.g., child care, if applicable to you). Every time you do, your supervisor gives you a hard time. And now, your supervisor has given you a written warning about it. It's unfair! You're angry—and frightened (you need to keep your job and you need to deal with these personal issues).

Coping with Someone Threatening You with a Weapon

The previous sections deal with how to de-escalate a *potentially* violent person. But what can you do when faced with actual violence, specifically when threatened with a weapon? Larry Chavez has provided a six-point guideline for this, as well:

1. **Quietly signal for help.** Use a duress alarm system (e.g., a panic button) or a code word. And have someone else call 911. (The sidebar describes Don Grimme's own brush with violence and how he dealt with it.)

In the fall of 1972, I was working for an employment agency on the top floor of an office building in the heart of midtown Manhattan. At 4:30 p.m. on a Friday afternoon, two gunmen walked off the elevator into the agency and proceeded to hold us up.

The first I became aware of it was when I looked up from a phone call I was on to see a gun pointed at my head. The gunman told me: "Shut up and put down the phone, you @#$%!"

My first impression, believe it or not, was that it was a toy gun. I said: "Go away. Don't bother me." (Note: That is *not* good defusing technique!) Fortunately, my three coworkers in that office area were not as clueless as I. They said: "Don, this is serious. Put down the phone." I did and we were all tied up.

We've inserted my story here, since, obviously, I was not in a position to pick up the phone again and dial 911. Fortunately, a coworker in another office area down the hallway heard the commotion and told the person with whom she was speaking on the phone: "Call the police. I think we're being held up!"

Twenty minutes later, two policemen entered our offices with their guns holstered to investigate a vague report. There was a gunfight in the hallway. We all scurried under our desks. One of the gunmen was killed. The other, after pursuit in a stairwell, was arrested. Fortunately, neither the policemen nor any of us employees was injured.

2. **Keep your cool—don't aggravate his rage.** Maintain eye contact but don't stare. Project calmness, although you may not be feeling calm. Do not raise your own voice. Use the body language and phrasing described in the defusing guidelines.

3. **Stall for time and personalize.** Create and sustain conversation, unless instructed otherwise by the perpetrator (as Don was). Keep repeating your name. Talk about your family. Connect as a fellow person. Use the listening and questioning techniques from less escalated situations, to the extent possible.

4. **Negotiate.** Try to get as many little yeses from the perpetrator as possible—preparing for point 6. Start with basic requests, for example, "Is it okay if I take a deep breath?" Request permission to take at least three steps away from the perpetrator.

5. **Respect the weapon, but focus on the person holding it.** Follow the instructions of the person with the weapon. (Do as we say, not as Don did.) Don't risk harm to yourself or others. Never attempt to disarm or accept a weapon from the person in question. Why do you think we say to not accept a weapon, even if offered voluntarily? If you are holding the weapon, it is still in play as a visible source of violence. And if someone else has called the police and they arrive on the scene, *you* will be perceived as the perpetrator. Instead, request that he place any weapons in a neutral location while you talk.

6. **Look for opportunities for getting yourself and others to safety.** For example, ask if uninvolved parties may leave the area—one of the significant negotiations toward which you've been building. Stay on the alert for a safe chance to escape. (In Don's story, they scrambled under their desks once the gunfire started.)

Coping with Telephone Threats

The situation is different when the threat is via phone:

- Keep calm. Keep talking . . . and listening.
- Don't hang up.
- Signal a coworker to get on an extension.
- Ask the caller to repeat the message and write it down.
- Repeat questions, if necessary.
- For a bomb threat, ask where the bomb is and when it is set to go off.
- Listen for background noises and write down a description.
- Write down whether it's a man or a woman; pitch of voice, accent; anything else you hear.
- Try to get the person's name, exact location, telephone number.
- Signal a coworker to immediately call the Federal Protective Service (FSP), a contract guard, or the local police.
- Notify your immediate supervisor.

Self-Protection Tips

Here are the most important tips for safely disciplining or terminating an employee:

1. Coordinate your decision and communications with an objective and consistent third party such as Human Resources (HR).
2. Preserve the involved employee's dignity. Never insult or demean the individual, even if he or she has violated policy or been a thorn in your side.
3. Whenever there is the slightest concern about a terminated employee becoming violent, have a second person present at the meeting. When terminating a male employee, at least one of the two people present should be male (preferably with a strong physical presence). Conduct the meeting near an exit and away from other employees. Do not allow the employee to return to the work area, at least not without a strong escort. Discourage/prohibit the employee from returning to any of your worksites.

4. When terminating a contract employee, confirm that the contract agency has effectively communicated termination. Otherwise, assume full responsibility for doing so safely.

How to Break Up a Fight

- Get assistance—intervening alone is dangerous.
- Remove the audience—onlookers fuel the fire.
- Avoid stepping between combatants—it shifts aggression to you.
- Try verbal intervention first—often combatants just need an excuse to stop.
- Use a distraction (loud noise, flickering lights)—this can break the intensity.
- Separate the combatants—break visual contact between them.

How to Protect Yourself While Shopping

- Avoid shopping alone. Try to shop with a friend or relative.
- Park your vehicle in a well-lighted area. Put radar detectors, cell phones out of sight.
- Know your surroundings. Keep an eye on the people in front and behind you.
- Carry your purse close to your body. Don't swing it. Don't flash large amounts of cash.
- Walk with confidence. Avoid talking to strangers.
- Approach your vehicle with your keys already in your hand.
- Don't carry too many packages. Place all packages out of sight (e.g., in the car trunk).
- Keep your car doors locked and your windows shut.
- If you see anything suspicious or it doesn't feel right, leave immediately; call the police.

How to Protect Yourself in a Parking Lot/Garage

- Leave only the ignition key with the attendant. Leave nothing with your name and address.
- Don't park next to a van's sliding door.
- Don't wear high heels when leaving work. Flats or sneakers are better to run in.
- Don't leave your workplace alone after dark. Leave in the company of others or with security.
- Approach your vehicle with your keys already in your hand.

- Look around for suspicious activity. If someone's loitering, walk past until they leave.
- Quickly scan your vehicle's interior (including the back seat) before unlocking the door.
- Keep your car doors locked and your windows shut.
- Be suspicious of anyone approaching you, even if asking for donations or with leaflets.

How to Protect Yourself While Walking at Night

- Avoid walking or running alone at night. Instead, walk or jog with a friend.
- Don't use headphones while walking, driving, or jogging.
- Always walk in well-lighted areas.
- Avoid the use of shortcuts.
- Keep away from large bushes or doorways where someone could be lurking.
- Always stay near the curb.
- Do not approach vehicles that stop to ask for directions. Answer from a distance.
- If followed, go immediately to an area with lights and people. If needed, change direction.
- Do not display cash openly, especially when leaving an ATM.

How to Protect Yourself against Domestic Violence

Employers should always be committed to working with employees who are victims of domestic violence to prevent abuse and harassment from occurring in the workplace. No employee should be penalized or disciplined solely for being a victim of harassment in the workplace. Establishments should provide appropriate support and assistance to employees who are victims of domestic violence. This includes confidential means for coming forward for help, resource and referral information, work schedule adjustments or leave as needed to obtain assistance, and workplace relocation as feasible.

Employees who are perpetrators of domestic violence should also be encouraged to seek assistance. Establishments should provide information regarding counseling and certified treatment resources, and make work-schedule arrangements to receive such assistance.

It is important that employers and employees know how best to respond to the effects of domestic violence in the workplace. In addition, they also should be aware of physical or behavioral changes in other employees and know whom—personnel officer, manager, and/or employee advisory service/

resource—they can contact for advice. They should not attempt to diagnose the employee.

The following are options for employees who are *victims* of domestic violence.

- Tell a trusted coworker, supervisor, or manager, and ask for help.
- Contact your personnel officer for assistance.
- Contact the Employee Advisory Service/Assistance resource.
- Call the local police.
- Notify your supervisor of a possible need to be absent. Find out what work schedule or leave options are available to you. Be clear about your plans to return to work and maintain communications with your supervisor during your absence.
- If appropriate and if safety is a concern, submit a recent photograph of the abuser and a copy of your protection order to your supervisor. This assists your employer in identifying the abuser should he or she appear in the workplace.

The following are options for employees who are *perpetrators* of domestic violence.

- Tell a trusted coworker, supervisor, or manager, and ask for help.
- Contact your personnel officer and ask for help.
- Contact the Employee Advisory Service/Resource.
- Obtain a referral to a certified domestic violence perpetrators' treatment program.

It is important that all employees know how best to respond to the effects of domestic violence in the workplace. Managers/supervisors or human resource professionals should receive domestic violence training. If an employee comes to you, as a manager, with information about domestic abuse, here are some steps to take:

- Be responsive when an employee who is either the victim or perpetrator of domestic violence asks for help.
- Maintain confidentiality. Information about the employee should only be given to others on a need-to-know basis.
- Work with the victim, personnel office, employee advisory service/resource, available security staff, law enforcement and community domestic violence programs, if necessary, to assess the need for and develop a workplace safety plan for the victim. Victims of domestic violence know their abusers better than anyone else. When it comes to their own personal safety, offer to assist

them in developing a workplace safety plan, but allow them to decide what goes in it. If it is determined that other employees or clients are at risk, it is essential to take measures to provide protection for them.

- Adjust the employee's work schedule and/or grant leave if the employee needs to take time off for medical assistance, legal assistance, court appearances, counseling, relocation. or to make other necessary arrangements to create a safe situation. Be sure to follow all applicable personnel rules.
- Maintain communication with the employee during the employee's absence. Remember to maintain confidentiality of the employee's whereabouts.
- Post information about domestic violence in your work area. Also, have information available where employees can obtain it without having to request it or be seen removing it, such as restrooms, lunchrooms, or where other employee resource information is located.
- Honor all civil protection orders. As appropriate, participate in court proceedings in obtaining protection orders on behalf of the employee.
- Maintain a list of services available to victims and perpetrators of domestic violence. This list should include employee advisory service/resource, local shelters, certified domestic violence treatment programs available to perpetrators, information about how to obtain civil orders of protection, and any available community resources.
- Advise and assist supervisors and managers in taking corrective or disciplinary actions against perpetrators of domestic violence.

Physical Security

Maintaining a physically safe workplace is part of any good prevention program. Many organizations have numerous security measures in place that can reduce the risk of workplace violence. These include employee photo identification badges, closed circuit cameras, silent alarms, metal detectors, two-way mirrors, electronic access systems, barriers to prevent cars from driving too close to the building, emergency internal code words, extra lighting in the parking lots, and escorts to and from parking lots after dark.

Planning groups should review security measures and procedures and make recommendations for modifications and improvements as necessary.

The following are ways to improve security in your office and/or building, suggested by the Federal Protective Service. (The following is excerpted from the Office of Personnel Management's website at www.opm.gov/Employment_and_Benefits/WorkLife/OfficialDocuments/handbooksguides/Workplace Violence/p3-s5.asp).

- Post a security guard at the main building entrance or at entrances to specific offices.

- Install a metal detector or CCTV (closed-circuit television) camera or other device to monitor people coming in all building entrances.
- Issue all employees photo identification cards and assign temporary passes to visitors, who should be required to sign in and out of the building. Under certain conditions, contract guards should be required to call . . . to confirm an appointment and/or to request an escort for all visitors—customers, relatives, or friends.
- Brief employees on steps to take if a threatening or violent incident occurs. Establish code words to alert coworkers and supervisors that immediate help is needed.
- Install silent, concealed alarms at reception desks.

The following are some examples provided by the FPS of ways to improve security in "front-line" offices that serve the public.

- Ensure that officers (or guards) have a clear view of the customer service area at all times.
- Arrange office furniture and partitions so that front-line employees in daily contact with the public are surrounded by "natural" barriers (desks, countertops, partitions) to separate employees from customers and visitors.
- Provide an under-the-counter duress alarm system to signal a supervisor or security officer if a customer becomes threatening or violent.
- Establish an area in the office for employees and/or customers to escape to if they are confronted with violent or threatening people.
- Provide an access-control combination lock on access doors.
- Mount closed-circuit television cameras for monitoring customer service activity from a central security office for the building.

For more detailed information about physical security, see appendix E.

Access Controls

Locks are the most acceptable and widely used security devices for protecting facilities, classified materials, and property. All containers, rooms, and facilities must be locked when not in actual use. Regardless of their quality or cost, locks are considered delay devices only. Some locks require considerable time and expert manipulation to open, but all locks can be defeated by force and with the proper tools. Locks must never be considered as a stand-alone method of security.

Turnstiles and revolving doors are access barriers that can be installed to continuously control and monitor every individual entering and or exiting a building. Whereas revolving doors are most often deployed to control the entry to a building from the street, turnstiles are usually set within the lobby of a building.

An ID system provides a method of identifying personnel. The system provides for personal recognition and the use of security ID cards or badges to aid in the control and movement of personnel activities.

Standard ID cards are generally acceptable for access into areas that are unrestricted and have no security interest. Personnel requiring access to restricted areas should be issued a security ID card or badge.

Procedures must be implemented to properly identify and control personnel. This includes visitors presenting their cards/badges to security at entrances of restricted areas. Visitors are required to stay with their assigned escort. Security must ensure that visitors stay in areas relating to their visit; an uncontrolled visitor, although conspicuously identified, could acquire information for which he is not authorized.

Duress Code

The duress code is designed to protect non-security personnel. If people see something suspicious, they must be trained to alert the proper authorities and not try to intervene themselves, which could put them and others in danger. For instance, a teacher who sees a stranger armed with a gun in the parking lot should not try to tackle the man but should use the duress code to summon help as quickly as possible.

The duress code is a simple word or phrase used during normal conversation to alert other security personnel that an authorized person is under duress. A duress code requires planning and rehearsal to ensure an appropriate response. This code is changed frequently to minimize compromise.

Two-Person Rule

The two-person rule is designed to prohibit access to sensitive areas or equipment by a lone individual. Two authorized persons are considered present when they are in a physical position from which they can positively detect incorrect or unauthorized procedures regarding the task or operation being performed. The team is familiar with applicable safety and access to sensitive areas or equipment that requires the two-person rule. When application of the two-person rule is required, it is enforced constantly by the personnel who constitute the team.

Computer Security

Planning groups should address ways to safeguard computer systems. There have been cases where employees have sabotaged computer equipment, com-

Security Equipment

- Utilize electronic alarm systems activated visually or audibly. Systems should identify the location of the room or location of the employee by means of an alarm sound and/or a lighted indicator or equally effective measure. Adequate personnel must be available to render prompt assistance if such systems are utilized.
- Utilize closed-circuit television cameras that permit security guards to monitor high-risk areas, both inside and outside the building.
- Utilize metal detection systems to identify persons with weapons.
- Utilize cell phones, beepers, CB radios, or handheld alarms or noise devices in field situations.
- Examine and maintain security equipment on a regular basis to ensure its effectiveness.

puter systems, and computer records. Therefore, whenever a risk of sabotage is suspected, procedures should be initiated to prevent the person from having access to the facility's computer system. It is important to act quickly whenever there is reason to believe that an employee or ex-employee may commit such an act. It is standard practice to collect IDs, building passes, keys, and parking passes when employees leave their jobs. Often, however, no one thinks to block access to computer systems or networks.

This type of access information is sometimes difficult to determine; often, it is not readily available in one central place. For example, information technology administrators may know who has access to various computer systems, and the facilities manager may know who has access to the computer systems that control the building's heating, air-conditioning, and other support functions for the facility. The planning group, as part of the response plan, should talk to the information/computer security officer or computer system administrators to determine the vulnerability of the computer networks and the procedures that need to be implemented to lock individuals out of these systems.

Law Enforcement

Depending on the organization, the location, and the type of incident or situation, jurisdiction may vary. The organization's own security or law enforcement organization (e.g., the Federal Protective Service [FPS] or federal, state, or local law enforcement), or a combination of these, may have jurisdiction. There also may be gaps in law enforcement coverage when issues of workplace violence arise. These gaps can be closed if the threat assessment team (which would include any in-house security organization) works with the various law enforcement organizations in setting up workplace violence programs. The following

Security Professionals
by Ryan Groom

Security guards are of paramount importance to the physical security of your employees, events, and facilities. Security guards need to be included in the overall protective blanket of the organization. Even when security guards are outsourced, they need to be an integral component of your security plan and not considered a separate function.

OUTSOURCING SECURITY GUARDS

Once you have decided your organizational needs for short- or long-term security guards, the complexity of the security requirements that the security guards will fulfill will need to be defined. Are the security guards required for a special event or as an addition to your ongoing physical security plans? The target of this section is to provide knowledge to help you decide what needs to be considered when hiring security guards. If your security requirements are very complex, an on-site assessment by a security professional is recommended. You may want to consider hiring an external security consultant to help you write and review the request for proposal (RFP) you will send to security guard contractors. When hiring an outside security consultant to help with the proposal, make sure the consultant does not have ties to any security guard staffing agencies so you can get unbiased third-party assistance.

The first decision to make is: whether you require security guards for the short term or long term. Long-term guards need to be deeply integrated into your security plan and be part of the security team. Short-term guards are needed for special events and times of heightened security. Hiring short-term guards usually means they are required for a particular function; that function needs to be defined and communicated perfectly to your short-term guards and the security guard agency.

It is important to remember that the guard has two major functions: first, to be present to deter and detect unusual or suspicious activity, and second, to safeguard property and people. How a security guard interacts with your organization is an indicator of how that security guard will follow policy and how members of your organization will respect the function of the security guards.

CRITERIA FOR SECURITY CONTRACTOR SELECTION

As soon as the need for a security firm has been determined on an immediate or long-term basis, a security contractor needs to be selected. Make sure you select a company that has a valid license. You should be certain that a company is reliable and in good standing.

All of the following criteria should be reviewed:

- adequate insurance
- reputation
- verifiable references
- experience and management
- training and qualifications
- staffing

- documentation
- equipment issues
- clear proposal
- costs
- contract

DECIDING WHAT KIND OF SECURITY GUARD SHOULD BE HIRED

Hiring security guards is serious business and should not be taken lightly. Various types of security guards are appropriate for different situations. One important issue is whether you would like security at your site to be provided by a uniformed or a plainclothes guard:

- The main goal for hiring a uniformed security guard is *deterrence*.
- The main goal for hiring a plainclothes security guard is *apprehension*.

After deciding what kind of security guard to hire, you must determine whether the security guard should be armed or unarmed. There are many costs and benefits to be considered when choosing armed versus unarmed security guards.

UNARMED SECURITY GUARDS

The majority of outsourced guards deployed are unarmed guards. In most situations, unarmed guards are effective. Unarmed security guards often provide the same deterrent as armed guards without the risk of deadly force. The protection afforded by unarmed guards is less expensive and may incur less liability and insurance. When selecting unarmed guards, consider:

- The use of deadly force is neither desired nor required.

ARMED SECURITY GUARDS

It is important to determine if hiring armed security guards meets your expectations for security. Armed guards may utilize deadly force. When selecting armed guards, consider:

- The training qualifications the security guards have with firearms.
- The contractor's policy on the use of weapons with regard to deadly force.
- Verifying references and making sure the reputation is a degree higher when hiring armed security guards.

Consider the cost-effectiveness of an armed guard. They are much more expensive than unarmed security, due to licensing and training requirements. Decide whether the presence of a weapon may escalate the possible use of force and violence which otherwise may not occur. Insurance may be adversely affected by the presence of an armed guard. An ineffectively deployed armed guard can pose additional risk to staff. Deploying armed guards should not be taken lightly but may be your only option if what you are protecting or the area that needs protection requires armed deterrents.

OUTSOURCING SUMMARY

Outsourcing security guards needs to be carefully decided. When hiring short-term security guards, the plan needs to be detailed and perfectly communicated to the short-term guards and your organization's staff. Security guards need to follow policy to the letter, and any deviation from the policy needs to be cleared with the guards' liaison. Security guards should not be chastised for following the policy to the letter. Deciding if the security guards should be armed or unarmed is a very important decision that can have noticeable ripple effects and sets a tone for the security posture of your organization.

When selecting security guards, nothing replaces experience and a great reputation.

CRITERIA FOR SECURITY CONTRACTOR SELECTION

Security personnel are necessary if you have to remove "undesirable" elements from your premises, such as disgruntled employees or even thieves and suspected criminals. Also, if you decide to hire armed guards, you have to be prepared for the use of deadly force and the fact that people could be harmed or killed on your premises.

Do not rush into hiring the first firm that has a nice uniform or a shiny badge. Get quotes in plenty of time to select a firm with a great reputation and track record to handle all of your security guard needs. The following items are issues to review in detail when selecting a security contractor.

Adequate Insurance and License

After you have established that a security contractor is duly licensed, scrutinize the insurance coverage the security contractor provides. Every jurisdiction that licenses security contractors keeps records on licensed security firms. Make sure you hire a company that has a valid, current license that covers your jurisdiction. An effective method to determine the reputation of the potential contractor is by investigating any history of complaints reported against it to the licensing authority.

The following insurance criteria should be met prior to hiring a security contractor:

- Your insurance agent approves of the coverage of the contractor.
- Liability insurance of the contractor covers a minimum of $1 million per incident and $3 million total. The higher the coverage the better.
- Determine whether the contractor has fidelity bonding and other coverage. Fidelity bonding is a business insurance policy that protects the employer in case of any loss of money or property due to employee dishonesty. It is like a guarantee to the employer that the person hired will be an honest worker.
- The contractor's workers compensation insurance is at jurisdictional minimums.
- The contractor should have adequate automobile liability insurance coverage for all vehicles used.
- The contractor's insurance should cover sexual harassment through its professional liability coverage.

- Liability coverage for any special equipment should be provided.
- The contractor's insurance carriers should name your organization as an "additional insured" on their liability insurance policies (or at least, obtain certificates of insurance for the contractor). This is especially important for long-term contracts.
- Your insurance advisor should not object to any policy exclusions.
- Ask for the contractor's employment modification rate (EMR) for the last three years. The lower the EMR, the better the contractor's safety performance.
- Request "loss experience" or "loss runs" reports from the contractor in order to review its history of liability insurance claims.
- Request the contractor's listing of workers compensation claims to determine the possibility of patterns of carelessness or inadequate employee safety practices.

Reputation

A security contractor's reputation should be examined to ensure that the company has maintained a trustworthy and dependable reputation. To determine the quality of past work, ascertain whether there has been a recent history of valid or successful lawsuits or complaints to agencies filed by clients or employees against the contractor. This can be determined at your local courthouse or through a local attorney. The items discussed in the "Adequate Insurance and License" section above will also help gauge the contractor's reputation.

Verifiable References

References help identify quality and reputable security contractors. Client references give invaluable insight as to the reliability and performance of a security contractor and highlight areas of possible improvement. Make sure you verify the references; a simple phone call to current and past clients will be very insightful. To help you pick the most qualified and experienced security firm, look at

- references from clients, which verify a contractor's history of relevant experience
- references from past clients, which verify a contractor's history
- references that indicate a contractor's employee turnover rate is lower than or equal to that of industry norms (Turnover rate for security guard contractors can be as high as 100 percent–300 percent per annum.)

Experience and Management

It is important to recognize that you are hiring the security guard contractor's management team. Given the high turnover rate for the security guard industry, this is extremely important, as the pool of security guards is the same for all companies. Inquire as to the number of years of service in the security industry of the contractor's president, regional manager, and operations management. Although not essential, the security contractor should have recently provided security service to an organization similar to yours.

- Discuss your requirements directly with the security company management.
- Discuss terms of how the security guard firm supervises field staff. Contractors should be willing to explain clearly how they will monitor and control the quality of security services.
- Determine the process of how a guard is performing below par will be counseled, disciplined, and replaced by the contractor.
- Require that all that written materials from the security guard (logs, reports, etc.) be clear, complete, and usable. You should receive a copy of every report filed by your guard.

Training and Qualifications

The proposal should define the minimum qualifications. Describe the security-related education, training levels, and experience of personnel that will be required for your organization. Security contractors that provide additional education and training to their staffs are preferable.

Staffing

Staffing may be regular, rotating, or temporary, and it is important to know beforehand which staffing requirements you will be dealing with. A permanent staff assignment is always best, if it can be obtained. However, security contractors often have difficulty maintaining regular staff as a result of odd shifts, frequently consisting of less than eight hours. You should research the security contractor's history of staff stability and be wary of excessive turnover or poor relationships with employees. The contractor should also obtain your approval before transferring (or replacing) personnel from your site. It is important to ensure that the contractor's needs at other sites not take precedence over security needs at your site.

Reporting

Request the frequency of reports and documentation (daily officer activity logs, incident reports, crime reports, officer time sheets, other special reports, etc.) that the guard generates for his employer; then determine how you would like this data reported to your organization. These reports need to flow smoothly into your organization's security team so they can be used for risk detection/escalation, security planning, and pattern recognition. Consistent and thorough written communication is an important output of contract security services and is an important management control mechanism you have over security services and costs.

Instructions to Security Guard

Carefully analyze whether the proposal includes sample post orders or a standard operating procedures manual that the guards abide by. This document describes all aspects of job performance at your site including security guard grooming and decorum, sets the standard of security services, and provides the basis of guard discipline. Ultimately, this document becomes the main basis of legal defense in the event of litigation.

Proposal Clearly Defined

Carefully analyze the proposal submitted by the security agency. The proposal should address the specific security needs at your site and demonstrate that the security contractor has carefully reviewed and considered your needs.

Costs

Prospective security contractors should address the following issues:

- How frequently will the contractor bill for services rendered? Weekly? Bi-weekly? Other? Is this convenient for you?
- Will it be a flat monthly rate, a uniform hourly rate for all employees, or a unique hourly rate for each individual employee? Generally, paying a unique hourly rate for each guard provides clients with the most economical and flexible service.
- The contractor should disclose wages to be paid to guards assigned to your site. A good contractor should be willing to discuss openly all cost drivers and the fee or profit margins it expects to earn for the services to be provided.
- The contractor's periodic invoices should list wages and bill rates for each guard. Invoice detail provides a good audit trail and shows contractor professionalism.
- How will guard pay increases be handled? Inadequate or stagnant wages are a frequent cause of staff turnover. Wage increases should be proposed in advance by the contractor especially for long-term contracts; increases should be based on officer incentive and merit, reflected logically in billing rate adjustment, and mutually agreed upon by the contractor and client before implementation.
- Will any additional charges be made for uniforms, equipment, supplies, etc.? Again, these should be proposed, justified, logical, and mutually agreed upon.
- Is the total estimated average monthly cost within your budget? Your monthly guard budget can be calculated by multiplying the hourly wage rate.

Contract

The security contract defines the rights and responsibilities between you and your contractor and ensures that the contractor will meet your needs. There are numerous questions and criteria that a security contract should specifically address in order to ensure that the security firm is responsible and dependable. Following is a list of guidelines to refer to:

- Does the contractor indemnify you for all security-related liability for which the contractor is responsible? In cases where partial liability is determined by a court of law, does the agreement clearly specify how such indemnifications shall be applied? You should discuss client indemnification of the contractor.
- At contract time will there be a price increase? How much? Why?
- Do you retain the right to terminate the agreement at any time and for any reason? Is this right mutual?

- Is the amount of notice required for contract termination—by the contractor or client—reasonable? Thirty days is the standard.
- Is the agreement sufficiently flexible to meet your needs?
- Does it assure fairness to the contractor and adequate control to the client?
- Can you replace a guard if necessary? For any reason?

Selecting a security contractor is not easy and should not be taken lightly, but by asking the right questions up front and reviewing the proposal based on the above criteria (and summarized in figure 3.3), you will be able to select the right security guard contractor for your organization.

The following checklist is to assist in the selection of a security guard contractor. Use one sheet for each contractor interviewed or per proposal reviewed. Assign rating and add comments to each category to score each security guard contractor to aid in selection.

Organization Name: _____

Department: _____

Date Assessed: _____

Contractor Name: _____

Item	Rating (1–10)	Notes
Adequate insurance and license		
Reputation		
Verifiable references		
Experience and management		
Training and qualifications		
Staffing		
Reporting		
Instructions to security guard		
Costs		
Contract		

Figure 3.3.   Criteria for hiring security contractors.

DEALING WITH SECURITY GUARDS

A security guard is required to deter and detect unusual or suspicious activity. The following are key points that the contact person should discuss with the security guard:

- assignment of a liaison from the organization to the security guard
- requirements of the assignment
- liaison contact and how to immediately reach him or her
- escalation procedures when danger is detected or being repelled
- special circumstances detailed
- purpose of security during the prescribed times (Define any times that heightened security may be required.)
- informing the security guard that he or she will be assessed during the shift for alertness
- rules of conduct that enhance effectiveness (e.g., guards need to be serious and professional)
- especially in highly sensitive locations, the need for separation of personal and professional conduct (No matter the rank of the person that might be violating policy, a guard must react as an act of policy no matter the violator. If a security guard does not enforce breach of policy, he or she will be ineffective.)
- layout of the facility
- facility security and/or fire regulations
- any vulnerable areas
- locations of telephones, firefighting equipment, fire alarms, emergency exits, etc.

COMMUNICATION SKILLS

Security personnel must exercise good interpersonal communication skills when carrying out their duties with other employees. Bad employee relations can result if security personnel become impertinent and assume powers not rightfully theirs. Security personnel must understand the methods and techniques that will detect security hazards and assist in identifying dangers.

Security officers with the assistance of law enforcement should be involved in all stages of the planning process in an effective workplace violence prevention program. They can play an active role in prevention, intervention, and response to dangerous situations, in addition to their traditional role of responding to actual incidents of physical violence.

are some suggestions for involving law enforcement in agency efforts to prevent workplace violence.

JURISDICTION

The team should identify which agencies have responsibility for its worksite. For example, the FPS is the primary law enforcement service for responding to incidents in federal facilities under the charge and control of the General

Services Administration (GSA) as an owned or leased facility. FPS typically locates its offices in areas where there is a high concentration of federal employees and is capable of providing timely responses to GSA-owned or leased facilities in these areas. For immediate responses to GSA-owned or leased facilities in rural areas and/or areas with a small federal presence, law enforcement officials from local jurisdictions should be contacted.

Some agencies have in-house security and/or law enforcement organizations. Others have contracts with private security firms. It is not always clear who has jurisdiction, and who should be contacted when the need arises.

Sometimes meeting with the local police chief, county sheriff, or state police is necessary to establish a plan or procedure regarding law enforcement response in the event of potential violence or hostile incidents. Sometimes new building agreements will be necessary or contracts will have to be modified. In remote locations, arrangements can be made for local police to handle certain situations.

The threat assessment team, and later the incident response team, should maintain open and continuous liaison with those law enforcement agencies responsible for their worksite. This would entail having periodic meetings to discuss concerns. Without these contacts, lines of communication can break down and misunderstandings can arise. It is during these contacts that the organization can obtain the names and telephone numbers of law enforcement personnel to be called upon should the need arise. Planning groups in organizations that already have established liaisons should work through these established liaisons to avoid confusion.

"What Would You Do If" Scenarios

Test your understanding of violence defusing and coping principles in the following scenarios. In each case, think about what you would do prior to reading our suggestions. Feel free to adapt or even challenge our suggestions. You may be able to come up with better responses, particularly as they apply to your environment or personal attributes (e.g., security or law enforcement expertise, self-defense training, gender, size and physical presence, personality, interpersonal skills, etc.).

SCENARIO 1: THE TIRED TRUCK DRIVER

A truck driver, coming in from a long distance, arrives at the loading dock to find his load not ready. He says he will sleep until the load is ready. You tell him the policy is that he cannot sleep on the property. He reacts aggressively.

Suggested Response: Your impulse probably would be to argue with him and enforce the policy. However, think about the possible consequences of that. He already is verbally aggressive and may very well become physically aggressive, if challenged. Also there is a good chance that he keeps some type of weapon in his truck. Balance those consequences with the consequences of allowing a temporary lapse in your policy. What impact will that lapse have on important things like productivity and safety? Probably not much.

Instead, look at the situation from his point of view. He arrives at your facility tired from a long drive. He's frustrated that his load is not ready. His proposed method of coping with the situation is reasonable: sleep. Then you tell him he can't do that, for what he would perceive to be an arbitrary reason.

So why not back off and let him sleep? Then, in safety, you can try to expedite the loading of his truck, contact senior management for guidance on resolution, notify security, and/or contact the police.

SCENARIO 2: THE STUBBORN SMOKER

You attempt to enforce the no-smoking rule in the employee break area. Smoky is a long-term employee who says, "I'll smoke where I want, when I want." He flips the cigarette butt at you and lights up again.

Suggested Response: His flipping a cigarette butt at you is an act of physical violence and should not be tolerated. However, enforcement of both your smoking rules and your violence policy are better left until *after* the immediate situation is resolved peacefully. His disobedience and this manner of violence are not yet dangerous to you or others.

Why not back off and notify the appropriate parties (e.g., Smoky's manager and HR) for implementation of disciplinary action.

If you are Smoky's manager or otherwise know him fairly well, you may want to inquire about his well-being. He is a long-term employee. It is unlikely that he is always this hostile. Apply the defusing guidelines, and not merely as a calming technique, but as a sincere and sympathetic listener to whatever is troubling him.

SCENARIO 3: THE DRUNKEN CONTRACTORS

Several individuals on a contractor crew drink their lunch. Upon returning from lunch, the contractors are stopped from entering the facility by the security officer at the employee entrance. Shouting, verbal insults, and pushing ensue.

Suggested Response: This is more challenging. In the first two scenarios, we recommended that you let the person have his way, at least temporarily. Here you cannot afford to do that. The consequences of letting these violent drunks enter your facility could be quite negative. On the other hand, aggressively prohibiting them from entering could escalate the already violent situation.

This is not a situation you should attempt to resolve alone. Apply the first point of the coping guidelines: quietly signal for help, using a duress alarm system. While you're waiting for help to arrive, utilize whatever physical security systems are in place to protect yourself and others, and apply the defusing guidelines.

Try a jovial approach, tapping into the silly side of their drunkenness. You want them to prefer spending time fooling around with you, rather than going back to work. Perhaps reassure them that returning late to their work stations is no big deal. Remember that their judgment is impaired.

Instead of being hostile or officious, perhaps be apologetic about your inability to let them into the facility. You're a guy or gal just like them who has to cope with "stupid" rules. Do a lot of grinning and shrugging, rather than glaring and arm crossing.

Once help arrives, see to it that the individuals are safely evicted from the facility and never return. Notify the contracting company, relevant internal personnel (e.g., security, HR, contractors' managers), and the police.

SCENARIO 4: HUNTING SEASON

It's hunting season. You've already stopped several employees from bringing hunting rifles and pistols into the facility. Now Hunter Hal refuses to part with his hunting knife at the employee entrance. So far (at least) Hal is calm, but he is being stubborn.

Suggested Response: Like the previous scenario, you cannot afford to let the individual have his way, but you can let him have his say. That is, prevent him from entering the facility, but let him talk. Don't attempt to disarm him. Your goal is to have him either voluntarily check his knife at the entrance or return to his vehicle and leave his knife there.

Since he is calm, you may want to try reasonable persuasion. Point out the rationale for the weapons policy (focusing your comments on the potential danger of the knife and not on him or his character) and listen to his point of view. Try to reassure him about his concerns and make helpful suggestions that would both meet his needs and safety requirements. Remain calm and friendly yourself, but quietly firm on your being unable to let the knife into the facility.

If he becomes hostile or more upset, quietly signal for help, refrain from persuasion, and apply the defusing techniques.

SCENARIO 5: THE JEALOUS HUSBAND

A married couple work different shifts. Suspicious Sam works second shift and Adulterous Adelle works first shift. Convinced that Adelle is having an affair with one of her coworkers (Romeo) during the hours that Sam is working, Sam takes a day off and comes to sit in the parking lot, intending to confront Adelle and Romeo.

Suggested Response: Greet Sam in a friendly manner and ask him why he's sitting in the parking lot (expressing mild curiosity, rather than suspiciousness). Apply the defusing guidelines and listen with interest, gently probing to get him to open up. Remind him (in a matter-of-fact way) of your anti-lingering policy and request that he leave.

If he does leave, notify Sam's manager and HR of Sam's actions (and of whatever may be relevant that you learned in your conversation with him). If he becomes defensive and aggressive, back off and (outside his presence) also notify security and/or the police.

Be ready to provide (from Step 4):

1. A description of Sam's vehicle: make, model, color, and license plate number
2. A physical description of Sam: age, weight, hair color and length, clothing, facial hair, and any other distinguishing features

If you know about the affair—or learn about it from Sam during your conversation with him—ensure that Adelle and Romeo are alerted to Sam's actions and whatever relevant statements he made to you.

SCENARIO 6: HEY, THERE'S A FIGHT!

Two employees are fighting on the factory floor. Another employee runs into the hall, stops you and asks that you do something about the fight.

Suggested Response: Apply the guidelines from "How to Break Up a Fight." That is, get assistance (from security or whomever is readily available) to isolate the combatants from other employees. Use nonphysical means to break the intensity and separate the fighters—e.g., verbal distractions like a noise, or flickering lights. If physical intervention is absolutely required, have trained individuals such as security approach each combatant from behind to restrain them.

Then, with the aid of another person, separately escort each combatant to enclosed offices for conversation with the individual's manager and/or Human Resources. Apply defusing techniques to calm each individual and to gain information about what led to the fight. Apply appropriate disciplinary action (which probably will entail termination of at least one of the combatants) and notify the police, certainly if anyone has been seriously injured.

SCENARIO 7: I'M FIRED?!

You have been asked to stand by during a termination. The HR rep, Penny Personnel, believes that the terminated employee, Hostile Harry, may react violently. And in fact he does—shouting and throwing things around Penny's office, next door to where you are waiting.

Suggested Response: Quickly call security and/or 911. Then knock on Penny's door and say something like "Is everything OK in there?"—loudly enough to be heard through the door, but without yelling. Pause to hear any response from Penny or Harry and/or a subsiding or increase in the shouting/throwing.

Then quietly enter the office, prepared to defend yourself, but maintaining a nonthreatening manner. (Be sure to close the door behind you.) Your very presence may be enough to stop Harry's tirade. Apply the defusing and coping techniques. Of course, your motivation is to protect Penny (and yourself), but present yourself as Harry's ally and advocate. Listen to his concerns; appear to persuade Penny to reconsider the termination or look into the possibility of doing so.

Once he has calmed and/or security or police arrive, see that he is escorted out of the facility and never returns. File criminal charges against Harry, certainly if he has injured anyone or damaged property.

In hindsight, it would have been better to have you in the same office with Penny, rather than next door.

Assess and Contain

An employer's workplace violence prevention program should designate the personnel who will be specifically responsible for overseeing and implementing the organization's antiviolence policy, including risk assessment and incident response. Teams should have the authority, training, and support needed to meet their responsibilities.

The risk assessment and incident response teams will be responsible for responding to *all* reports of violence, threats, harassment, or other events or conduct that may frighten any employee. Often, team members will receive special training in risk evaluation, threat assessment, conflict resolution, and procedures to monitor, document, and develop a response to all cases brought to their attention. They also need to be aware of, and have contingency plans for, issues such as dealing with the news media in the event of a major incident and helping meet employees' needs in the aftermath of a violent death or other traumatic workplace event.

It should be explained that, often, these teams will not conduct threat assessments themselves, but instead will seek the assistance of outside threat assessment professionals to perform the function with the team's collaboration.

Teams often will benefit from consulting with law enforcement officials, mental health professionals, emergency response personnel, and other outside specialists or agencies that could become involved in a crisis. To be fully effective, these relationships should be established and maintained *before* an emergency occurs.

The composition of assessment and response teams will reflect a multidisciplinary approach. Teams often include representatives from security, HR, medical, and employee assistance in organizations large enough to have those departments.

Other possible members are union representatives, where employees are covered by a union contract. While team members may belong to different departments, as a team, they should report to one senior manager, so that lines of communication and authority are clear and there will not be conflict or confusion in the midst of an emergency. The team's composition, tasks, and powers should be clearly defined. Employers may want to hire outside experts to train and advise the assessment and incident response teams. Those teams, in turn, can conduct violence prevention and emergency response training for employees, supervisors, and executives.

Teams should keep good written records of all incidents and interventions, monitor results, and evaluate the actions that were taken.

Risk Assessment Team

The risk assessment team should be designated to assess the vulnerability to workplace violence and reach agreement on preventive actions to be taken. The team should also be responsible for

- recommending/implementing employee training programs on workplace violence
- implementing plans for responding to acts of violence
- communicating internally with employees

Risk assessment team membership should include representatives of the following:

- senior management
- employee assistance program
- operations/department managers
- employees or their representatives
- security personnel
- public relations experts
- medical personnel
- law enforcement
- legal advisors
- background investigators
- HR
- violence assessment experts
- finance
- conflict resolution

The following section, excerpted from the *OSHA Handbook on Workplace Violence*, provides a more detailed description of the responsibilities of various persons or offices.

EMPLOYEES

While not necessarily on the risk assessment team, employees do have responsibilities.

- Be familiar with the organization's policy regarding workplace violence.
- Be responsible for securing the workplace.
- Be responsible for questioning and/or reporting strangers to supervisors.
- Be aware of any threats, physical or verbal, and/or any disruptive behavior of any individual and report such to supervisors.
- Be familiar with local procedures for dealing with workplace threats and emergencies.
- Do not confront individuals who are a threat.
- Be familiar with the resources of the Employee Assistance Program.
- Take all threats seriously.

MANAGERS AND SUPERVISORS

- Inform employees of organization's workplace violence policies and procedures.
- Ensure that employees know specific procedures for dealing with workplace threats and emergencies, and how to contact police, fire, and other safety and security officials.
- Ensure that employees with special needs are aware of emergency evacuation procedures and have assistance (as necessary) regarding emergency evacuation situations.
- Respond to potential threats and escalating situations by utilizing proper resources from the following: local law enforcement and medical services, Federal Protective Service, HR staff, and the Employee Assistance Program (EAP).
- Take all threats seriously.
- Check prospective employees' backgrounds prior to hiring.
- Coordinate with other co-located agencies to develop joint workplace violence prevention plans.

ORGANIZATION'S HEADS

- Develop a policy statement that indicates the organization will not tolerate violent or disruptive behavior and that all reports of incidents will be taken very seriously and dealt with appropriately.

- Ensure that the *USDA Handbook on Workplace Violence Prevention and Response* as well as appropriate in-house materials are available to all employees and that all employees are aware of the procedures and instructions in them.
- Ensure that appropriate safety and law enforcement personnel have completed an on-site review of safety and security of buildings and offices.
- Provide adequate resources for employee training and awareness.
- Include workplace violence training in all employee orientation and supervisory training sessions.
- Provide funding for appropriate safety and security of employees.
- Ensure that performance standards of appropriate staff reflect the importance of workplace safety and security.
- Provide for briefings on workplace violence at staff meetings.

HUMAN RESOURCES STAFF

- Provide for supervisory training that includes basic leadership skills, such as setting clear standards of conduct and performance, addressing employee problems promptly, and using the probationary period, performance counseling, discipline, alternative dispute resolution, and other management tools conscientiously.
- Provide technical expertise and consultation to help supervisors determine what course of administrative action is most appropriate in specific situations.
- Determine whether sufficient evidence exists to justify taking disciplinary action once the investigation of any misconduct is complete.
- Help supervisors determine proper reasonable accommodation.

EMPLOYEE ASSISTANCE PROGRAM COUNSELORS

- Provide short-term counseling and referral services to employees at no cost.
- Assist with early involvement in organizational change.
- Train employees in dealing with angry coworkers and customers, conflict resolution, and communication skills.
- Train supervisors to deal with problems as soon as they surface, without diagnosing the employee's problem.
- Consult with supervisors to identify specific problem areas, develop action plans to resolve problems in the early stages, and encourage employees to contact the EAP for individual counseling.
- Consult with incident response teams when a potential for violence exists or an actual incident is reported.
- Participate on critical incident stress debriefings teams in the event of a violent situation.

UNIONS/EMPLOYEE ORGANIZATIONS

- Be familiar with and actively support policy and contract language on workplace violence prevention.
- Stay alert to security issues and potential threats.
- Stay fully abreast of procedures for addressing workplace threats and emergencies.
- Stay fully abreast of the Employee Assistance Program, including the procedures/policy regarding the ability of designated union officials to make employee referrals to EAP.
- Work closely with all levels of management to ensure that employees are up to date on the organization's workplace violence prevention policy and procedures.
- Participate fully with management in all phases of workplace violence prevention and response, including membership on threat assessment and incident response teams.

SECURITY/FACILITIES STAFF

- Serve as the liaison with law enforcement as well as the local expert on security matters.
- Conduct regular threat assessment surveys of the facility to determine the level of security preparedness and any gaps in the security posture.
- Serve as the facility security expert, keeping management advised of the risk of violence, the security gaps identified by threat assessments, and the means to close these gaps, including the latest technologies.
- Work with facility personnel to improve the security level of the buildings, grounds, parking lots, and so forth.
- Train facilities personnel in security measures and violence prevention techniques. Facilities personnel should work closely with security staff to ensure that buildings, areas, and grounds are safe for employees and visitors. This includes not only keeping buildings and grounds well maintained but participating with security personnel in threat assessment surveys, keeping management informed of the status of the physical plant, and providing budget requests with justification for security upgrades.

LAW ENFORCEMENT STAFF

- Identify in advance the types of situations that may occur and when and how law enforcement should be notified of an incident.
- Indicate whether law enforcement officers have jurisdictional restrictions and identify alternative law enforcement agencies that may be able to provide assistance.

- Indicate whether law enforcement officers have arrest authority.
- Provide threat assessment personnel who can assist the organization in determining the best way to protect personnel.
- Suggest safety and security measures that need to be implemented.
- Arrange for all-employee briefings or training on specific workplace violence issues.

CONFLICT RESOLUTION OFFICERS

- Provide mediation and other alternative dispute resolution (ADR) services to assist employees in resolving disputes.
- Provide training in conflict resolution, communication, and negotiation skills

For more information go to www.usda.gov/news/pubs/violence/wpv .htm#five.

Conduct a Risk Assessment

A risk assessment is a survey of your vulnerabilities and criticalities and current state of readiness with recommendations for improvement that meet your particular culture, vision/mission, values, area, budget, and history. It should include

1. Conventional security measures.
2. A means to safely communicate a threatening situation. In some cases, that may take the form of duress alarms.
3. Policies that clearly state the organization's stand on violent, disruptive, and threatening behavior, as well as weapons in the workplace.
4. An incident reporting and tracking process that allows you to identify trends and vulnerabilities that may not otherwise be obvious.
5. An alternative reporting process in case the conventional channels and chains of command fail or aren't trusted. This may take the form of an ombudsman-type of manager or an internal or external hotline—all with confidentiality safeguards.
6. Clear and consistent commitment and demonstration by management to a safe workplace and to a culture of civility and respect.
7. A hiring process that screens out the potentially violent or unstable. Past behavior is the best predictor of future behavior, and background screens, personality inventories/testing, and proper interviewing are worthwhile tools. For example, the "loner" who couldn't get along with his or her former supervisors and peers probably won't get along in your organization, either.
8. Discipline, termination, and lay-off processes that, above all, preserve the involved employees' dignity. These should include the tactful and safe han-

dling of high-risk employees and situations. We are astonished by the organizations that still terminate with the guard escort parade past the employee's former peers—a practice just short of a public flogging.

9. Training of supervisors and managers on proper discipline and terminations (sometimes best handled by an objective, non–emotionally involved, third party such as HR), the early signs of a dangerous employee or situation, their duty to report, how to de-escalate threatening situations, their role in response and crisis management, and their responsibility to treat all people with respect and dignity.

10. Training of employees on awareness and reporting processes. It has been found that the most common thread found among attacks is that some or even many fellow employees were aware that the attacker was somehow unstable, had made threats, or discussed his or her plans before the incident. Likewise, such "leakage" was found following school attacks. Employees must understand that reporting such circumstances is not "squealing," but protects them and their fellow employees as well as the disruptive or troubled employee. Employees should also be encouraged to maintain an attitude of protectiveness for their work area and fellow employees. Like a Neighborhood Watch, this can be one of the most powerful overall security measures.

11. Employee Assistance Program (EAP) or other employee referral and support process. It is always best to aid the troubled employee before he or she becomes the threatening or violent employee. The EAP and its staff may also be very beneficial partners following an incident.

12. A crisis management program that includes a response team, counseling and investigative resources, emergency notification/evacuation process, media handling, family and community support, law enforcement liaison, and so on.

13. Periodic testing of the systems and processes. Most security and protection programs only fail upon being tested.

14. Ongoing reviews and assessments of the program to ensure continuing readiness.

See the detailed risk assessment checklist at the end of this chapter for specific issues to address during your risk assessment.

Incident Response

Assemble an incident response team that includes

- senior management
- Employee Assistance Program

- department managers
- public relations experts
- security personnel
- local law enforcement
- medical personnel
- Human Resources

Create an incident response plan that addresses

- policy
- public relations plan
- procedures
- logistics plan
- team members and roles
- professional contacts
- communication plan
- recovery plan

This plan should include detailed procedures—supported by training and rehearsal—specifying who does what and when. For example:

- how to restrain the perpetrator (and when to do so)
- dealing with the perpetrator after the incident
- how to contain the incident, and evacuation protocols
- notification of security staff and/or police
- summoning of medical staff
- communications—during the incident and afterwards
- providing EAP support

Incident Response Planning

EMERGENCY PLANS

Many offices already have emergency plans (also called incident/crisis response plans) that describe procedures to follow during a fire or other emergency. Most, however, do not cover workplace violence emergencies, including bomb threats. These plans should also include violent incidents. The plan should be specific to the type of facility, building, and the workers it covers, and it should describe

- procedures for calling for help
- procedures for calling for medical assistance
- procedures for notifying the proper authorities or whomever is acting in their place, security personnel, and the police

- emergency escape procedures and routes
- safe places to escape, inside and outside the facility
- procedures to secure the work area where the incident took place
- procedures for accounting for all employees if a facility is evacuated
- procedures for identifying personnel who may be called upon to perform medical or rescue duties
- training and educating employees in workplace violence issues and the emergency action plan
- procedures for regularly evaluating and updating the plan
- procedures for debriefing participants to identify lessons learned

IMMEDIATE RESPONSE TO A SEVERE INCIDENT

When a severe incident occurs in the workplace, the following procedures are to be followed immediately:

- If possible, remove or warn other potential victims.
- Move to a safe area.
- Call for immediate assistance:
  - other staff in immediate vicinity
  - police
  - ambulance
  - contact team
  - people in position of responsibility
- Do not attempt to physically stop the offender by stepping between the offender and the person or property he or she is attacking. Do not attempt to restrain the person unless it is a life-threatening situation and there are no other options. It normally takes four or five people to restrain an angry person without damage to themselves or the person and must only be attempted by people with the correct training.
- Remove or secure potential weapons (e.g., knives).
- Secure the environment (e.g., if seeking refuge in a room, lock doors and windows).
- Attend to first-aid needs.

RESPONSE WHEN IMMEDIATE DANGER HAS CEASED

The guidelines below provide assistance when the violence and abuse has ceased.

- Maintain safety and support of victim and offender where appropriate.
- Attend to first aid.
- Monitor behavior of offender, if possible.

- Call for assistance:
  - after-hours contact team
  - manager
  - external organizations
- Implement behavior management program if appropriate.
- Document in brief an outline of the incident, noting the time the incident occurred, venue, witnesses, offender, victim, possible cause, and action taken.

FOLLOW-UP

- Secure property and premises if needed.
- Report to appropriate managers.
- Follow-up medical examination if needed.
- Organize follow-up debriefing.
- Re-establish routine, if possible.

Workplace Evacuation Plan—Getting Everyone Out! by Ryan Groom, About.com

bizsecurity.about.com/od/buildingsecurity/a/Evacuation.htm

EVALUATION

Each workplace is different from the last so the specifics will also vary. The first step in a sound plan is evaluation. Remember when you had to invite the boring security guys in to do a risk assessment? Part of that risk assessment would involve emergency planning. You as a business need to be as prepared as possible for the unknown. Events such as fire, flood, chemical spills, terrorism, riots, and workplace violence are all things that need to be considered. Ultimately the plan is designed to allow a business to carry on business in the light of unforeseen activities. No small feat. Once you have identified the disasters, you need to start discussing personnel assignments. Who will be in charge of which scenario? Who will be the redundant person in case something happens to the primary? Involve management so that they understand the process and can contribute information to scenarios you may not have thought about. Management's main objective is to ensure continuity of the business (after safety of the staff, of course).

DRAWING UP THE PLAN

In the Canadian government, they have what are called standing orders (SO). These SO are posted and include information on hazardous materials, first aid, and any other pertinent information employees should be aware of. Your plan should be the SO for your organization.

1. You will need to develop a reporting mechanism for emergencies. Having the CEO running around, arms flailing, screaming that there is a fire in the kitchen is confusing and wholly ineffective. Decide who reports to whom.

2. Ensure you have an escape route and assignments. Ensure that there is a floor marshal whom everyone knows. Ensure that the floor marshal understands his or her responsibilities and (more importantly) is capable of executing them.

3. Have a fan-out list of phone numbers and addresses so that in an emergency everyone can get ahold of the people they need to. Who works where? Include contacts of people outside of the company.

4. Who performs what business task in the event of a disaster? With so much critical information, it may be pertinent for certain aspects of the company to remain secure even under situations of duress. There must be a process in place for critical systems to be shut down properly. Computers should be locked and rooms secured (if required to be secured).

5. Storage needs to be located off-site, so that the company can be up and running as quickly as possible with little interruption. This was evident in the aftermath of the World Trade Center bombings, when many organizations that had no off-site storage ceased to exist.

6. Ensure that people understand what alarms mean and how to react to them. A recent survey conducted by the National Research Council stated that almost 45 percent of those surveyed could not distinguish a fire alarm from other types of alarm. Twenty-five percent ignored the alarms, thinking it was a drill. Educate your staff.

7. Users should be aware of exactly what constitutes an emergency. Having users suddenly start shredding documents because Joe from Accounting left his toast too long in the toaster is not going to make anyone happy. Communication is the key.

8. Concerning medical staff: Who is licensed to perform first aid at your site? Where are the first-aid kits located? Who has the contact numbers for the hospital? All of these should be addressed in your plan.

9. Once it is determined that staff must leave the building, you need a process in place for accounting of people, specific and backup routes for evacuation, and assistance for people with disabilities. I once was involved in a fire at a youth group. One of the other leaders grabbed his child and left the area. Unfortunately, he was the person responsible for counting heads. It was only because another father had seen him leave with his son that we were able to account for everyone and not have to go back inside the burning building to search for him. People react differently in different situations. Build redundancy into your plan.

10. Lastly, practice the evacuation. Too often management does not see the benefit of conducting such procedures and sees them as a waste of time. The more people understand what is to happen during the practices, the more they will react properly in the actual situation.

For more information on creating a template for your evacuation plan, go to www.ready.gov/america/_downloads/sampleplan.pdf.

Hopefully, your evacuation plan will never be used. Develop and practice the plan as required. Remember, the plan is a living document and will constantly change.

Violence Response Protocols

A serious act of violence may be defined as an incidence of violence or potential violence that poses an imminent danger. The personal safety and security of the workforce must be of the greatest importance. The following response protocols are designed as guidelines to help you respond appropriately in situations that compromise your personal safety.

RESPONSE PROTOCOL: DANGEROUS OR ARMED PERSON

If you witness an armed individual at any time:

- Do not approach the person. Try to remain calm.
- If possible, notify someone immediately. Give your location, name, and reason for calling. Be ready to provide a physical description of the individual: age, weight, hair color and length, clothing, facial hair, and any other distinguishing features.
- If the individual is in a vehicle, attempt to get the vehicle's make, model, and color as well as the license plate number, if possible. Maintain your own safety.

If an armed suspect is outside your building:

- Move to an inner area of the building if safe to do so, and remain there until an "all clear" instruction is given by an authorized known voice.
- Turn off all the lights and close and lock all windows and doors. Close all window blinds and curtains.
- If you can do so safely, get all individuals on the floor and out of the line of fire.

If an armed suspect is inside the building:

- If it is possible to flee the area safely and avoid danger, do so.
- If flight is unsafe or impossible, lock all doors and secure yourself in your space.
- Close all window blinds and curtains.
- Contact security with your location, if possible.
- Get down on the floor or under a desk and remain silent.
- Get individuals on the floor and out of the line of fire.
- Wait for the "all clear" instruction.

If an armed suspect comes into your workplace office:

- There is no specific procedure that can be recommended to ensure your safety in this situation.

- Attempt to get the word out to other staff if possible. Call 911 or security, if possible.
- Put distance between yourself and the offender. Make use of shielding, if possible (e.g., a desk or filing cabinet between you and the offender).
- Do not challenge the offender. If flight is impossible, attempt to negotiate with the individual.
- If possible, keep an escape route behind you.
- Demonstrate an interest in solving the problem. Attempt to communicate to the individual that your main goal is to *help* them, not hinder them.
- Observe, listen, and take notes if appropriate.
- If the offender leaves your area, lock your door immediately. Remain in the area (unless your safety is in jeopardy), and await further instructions from authorities.

RESPONSE PROTOCOL: SUSPICIOUS INDIVIDUAL

Report any suspicious individual or activity. Give your location, name, and reason for calling. Be ready to provide a physical description of the individual: age, weight, hair color and length, clothing, facial hair, and any other distinguishing features. If the individual is in a vehicle, attempt to get the vehicle's make, model, and color as well as the license plate number, if possible. Follow the instructions provided to you by security.

RESPONSE PROTOCOL: SITUATIONS WHERE IMMEDIATE ACTION IS NOT REQUIRED

If you are concerned that a violent incident may occur, but immediate action is not required, contact security or the police. All reported incidents or threats of violence will be taken seriously. Reports will be investigated promptly and appropriate action taken. The risk assessment team will be convened as necessary and is responsible to

- ensure security is immediately provided and all appropriate parties are notified
- ensure a comprehensive investigation, acquiring appropriate resources where necessary
- investigate and assess the risk posed by the circumstance
- plan and implement a risk abatement action plan as necessary
- determining the appropriate interventions
- oversee necessary debriefings
- document
- take any action to prevent a similar situation from occurring in the future

RESPONSE PROTOCOL: EMERGENCY EVACUATION

It is important to be familiar with the nearest designated building exit for your area, as well as the location of the nearest fire extinguisher. Fire alarms should be tested on a regular basis. Fire drills should be performed on a regular basis and everyone must take part. Everyone must know the difference between the fire alarm drill alert and an evacuation alert.

The following procedure must be followed in case of an emergency evacuation of the building. When the fire alarm sounds:

- Everyone in the building must immediately evacuate the building in as orderly fashion as possible, using the predetermined (closest) exits.
- Take into consideration equipment shutoff, and so on.
- Supervisors are responsible to evacuate those in their charge.
- Each floor should have designated personnel to direct the evacuation as quickly as possible in a safe and controlled manner.
- Do not use the elevators unless you have received specific authorization to do so.
- If there are special needs persons in the building, one or two people should be assigned to assist them to evacuate or to stay with them in a safe place until the fire department arrives. Do not leave them alone.
- All building personnel and visitors will follow the instructions when asked to evacuate the building.
- *No one* shall reenter the building following a fire or fire drill until permission has been given by the Fire Department or a senior manager. The silencing of alarm bells is *not* an all-clear sign to reenter the building.
- If you suspect someone was not evacuated or you have any information about the incident that prompted the alarm, report it immediately.

RESPONSE PROTOCOL: BOMB THREATS

- The majority of bomb threats are made with the intent of disrupting normal business. However, every bomb threat must be investigated to ensure the safety of building occupants.
- If you have received a bomb threat, call the police or security. Be prepared to provide information from the Bomb Threat Check Sheet (included at end of this chapter). Follow the instructions you receive from the police or security.
- If you are told to leave the building, leave by the nearest and safest exit.
- When leaving, remove personal property such as purses, lunch containers, briefcases, and so on. Make a quick visual sweep of your area for any unusual items.

- *Do not touch anything suspicious—report any suspect object to security and/or police.*

PLAN YOUR ENCOUNTER WITH A POTENTIALLY VIOLENT PERSON

- If you know that you may be meeting with a potentially violent person, ensure a thorough threat assessment is conducted *before* you deal with the person. Try to determine what kind of behavior you can expect. This will help you to plan appropriate security measures. Don't assume everything will go safely. Denial and under-preparation are common factors in violent situations. Think through all the "what-ifs" and how you will respond.
- Plan a prepared script and try to keep to it.
- Don't conduct the encounter alone. Notify other staff if you anticipate trouble.
- Prepare your environment. Don't allow yourself to get into a situation where you have no way out. Position yourself so that you can see who is entering. Do not sit with your back to the door.
- Remove any items from the room that could be immediately dangerous or easily thrown (scissors, letter opener, heavy paperweight, etc.). Make sure you are the one closest to the door, not the person you are meeting with.
- Don't wear clothing items that could easily be used to choke you, such as a necktie, jewelry, scarf, and so forth.
- If you have speed dial, program it for security or the police. Ensure you have a communication system in place.
- Establish a recognizable signal with other staff that indicates you need assistance. Plan ahead of time with other staff what the appropriate responses should be.
- Mentally prepare yourself for blame, rage, personal insults, and other verbal assaults, and how you will respond appropriately.
- Treat the person with respect and sensitivity. Try to build up their dignity. Avoid raising your voice, arguing, questioning their integrity, staring, and condescending tones. Insensitivity strips the last of the person's dignity at a time when he or she is already feeling unstable. If this happens, the person may then feel totally justified in attacking.
- Prepare for the worst. Trust your instincts. Listen to your internal warning signs.

PERSONAL SAFETY TIPS

- Be aware of your surroundings. Know your emergency exits and procedures.

- Familiarize yourself with policies and procedures for your department and for the organization.
- Visualize ahead of time the appropriate responses to various situations that may arise.
- Trust your instincts. If you don't feel comfortable with a situation, get out of it!
- If you feel you are being harassed, threatened, intimidated, or are the victim of inappropriate behavior: Tell the person to stop. Document the incident. Inform your supervisor.
- If there is someone in your work area whom you don't recognize, ask if you can help him or her. Try to find out why he or she is there.
- Always lock your office when you leave, even if you are only leaving for a minute.
- Do not get into an elevator with anyone who makes you feel uneasy, or get off the elevator as soon as possible, whether you are at your floor or not.
- If you are working late at night, use the buddy system. Work in pairs. Have someone escort you to your car.
- Try to stay in well-lit, higher traffic areas.
- Have your keys ready when approaching your vehicle, and check the back seat prior to getting in.
- Know locations for telephones and have emergency numbers readily available.

The Aftermath

Despite the best-laid plans, violence in the workplace can and does happen. Just as organizations develop policies and procedures designed to head off these occurrences, they must be equally prepared to deal with the aftermath of such incidents. Quite often management's focus will be on getting the operational side of the office back in working order. However, just as important as getting the office back online is attending to the impact such incidents can have on office personnel.

Debriefing is used to minimize the psychological impact of a traumatic incident on victims, survivors, and relatives and generally is provided by trained mental health professionals. Employee Assistance Programs usually have counselors who specialize in this area. Local police departments and professional psychologists may also be available to assist. Debriefing entails individual or group sessions to discuss the incident and the impact it has had on people. Encouraging people to talk about the event as soon as they are comfortable doing so helps to lessen the psychological trauma resulting from the event. Some employees may never resume work at a site that has had a death or violent incident. These individuals may need counseling, outplacement services, or reassignment to another facility.

DEAL WITH THE AFTERMATH

- Address your employees' reactions.
- Address your managers' concerns.
- Gather professional support.
- Arrange for proper communication.
- Reassess and improve preventive measures.

According to the FBI's *Workplace Violence* handbook:

The effects of violence do not disappear after the violent act is over, and the harm is not only to the person directly attacked. A workplace violence prevention program should take into account that other employees, not just the victim, are affected and will need healing after a violent event—and that healing may come more easily if psychological support is part of an employer's crisis response from the beginning.

Emotional distress is potentially contagious, self-sustaining, and self-amplifying. Early intervention can slow or prevent the contagion. In the immediate aftermath of a crime, disaster, or other troubling incident, emergency psychological service can offer victims and their coworkers comfort, information, support, and help with practical needs. It can also spot those who appear most troubled by the event and [who] may need more intensive psychological attention in the future.

Information is crucial in controlling emotional distress during a crisis. When people don't know what is happening, they feel helpless, and when there is no solid news, rumors—often frightening ones—will fill the gap. Crisis managers need reliable information to make decisions. It is just as important for managers to share information with the rest of the workplace community as rapidly and honestly as possible, so that false reports and irrational fears do not spread and make the crisis worse.

As with all other aspects of emergency management, timely psychological support will be more effective if it has been prepared and practiced as part of an employer's workplace violence prevention plan. Planning cannot anticipate every circumstance, but a plan should identify those inside or outside a company who will direct and carry out the psychological support effort in a crisis. It should establish lines of communication and lay out alternative means of assembling employees as soon as possible once they are out of physical danger, for preliminary "debriefing" individually, in small groups, or in a large group.

Long-term psychological support may also be needed by victims and their coworkers after a serious episode of violence. (The following passage comes from the OSHA's guidelines for health and social service workers, but is applicable to employees in all occupations.)

All workplace violence programs should provide comprehensive treatment for victimized employees and employees who may be traumatized by witnessing a workplace violence incident. Injured staff should receive prompt treatment and psychological evaluation whenever an assault takes place, regardless of severity.

Victims of workplace violence suffer a variety of consequences in addition to their actual physical injuries. These include short- and long-term psychological trauma; fear of returning to work; changes in relationships with coworkers and family; feelings of incompetence, guilt, and powerlessness; and fear of criticism by supervisors or managers. Consequently, a strong follow-up program for these employees will not only help them to deal with these problems but also help to prepare them to confront or prevent future incidents of violence.

Several types of assistance can be incorporated into the post-incident response. For example, trauma-crisis counseling, critical incident stress debriefing, or employee assistance programs may be provided to assist victims. Certified employee assistance professionals, psychologists, psychiatrists, clinical nurse specialists, or social workers could provide this counseling, or the employer can refer staff victims to an outside specialist. In addition, an employee counseling service, peer counseling, or support groups may be established.

In any case, counselors must be well trained and have a good understanding of the issues and consequences of assaults and other aggressive, violent behavior. Appropriate and promptly rendered post-incident debriefings and counseling reduce acute psychological trauma and general stress levels among victims and witnesses. In addition, such counseling educates staff about workplace violence and positively influences workplace and organizational cultural norms to reduce trauma associated with future incidents.

Both early intervention and long-term healing efforts should avoid a one-size-fits-all approach. Not everyone will have the same emotional reaction or the same needs in the aftermath of a traumatic event, even if their experiences have been similar. Counselors should not press their services on employees in ways that may reinforce their identity as "victims." Rather, post-crisis psychological support should employ a variety of methods along the continuum of mental health care—including "getting out of the way" of those who may not want or need any intervention beyond an initial debriefing.

CRITICAL INCIDENT STRESS MANAGEMENT

The following section is taken from the U.S. Office of Personnel Management's *Dealing with Workplace Violence.*

Critical incident stress management (CISM) represents an integrated system of services and procedures whose purpose is to achieve several goals:

- prevention of traumatic stress
- mitigation of traumatic stress
- intervention to assist in recovery from traumatic stress
- acceleration of recovery whenever possible

- restoration to function
- maintenance of worker health and welfare

A CISM team, generally comprised of mental health professionals and trained peer support personnel, provides a variety of services, including

- defusings
- demobilizations after a disaster
- debriefings
- informal discussions
- significant other support services
- individual consults (one-on-one)
- follow-up services

For the purposes of this discussion, the focus will be on two of the more commonly used CISM services: debriefings and defusings.

Debriefings

The impact of a critical incident on an individual's life appear to be mitigated, to some degree, by the availability of resources that may intervene at various stages following the incident.

The critical incident stress debriefing (CISD) is a model designed to yield just such a result. The CISD model assists the victims of critical incidents with their recovery process.

The model incorporates seven phases:

1. Introductory Phase
2. Fact Phase
3. Thought Phase
4. Reaction Phase
5. Symptom Phase
6. Teaching Phase
7. Re-entry Phase

Debriefings are group meetings that are designed to give participants an opportunity to discuss their thoughts and feelings about a distressing event in a controlled and rational manner, and to help them understand that they are not alone in their reactions to the incident. It is recommended that a formal debriefing be held within twenty-four to seventy-two hours after an incident. Depending on the number of participants and the severity of the incident, debriefings generally last anywhere from one to three hours.

Debriefing teams represent a partnership between mental health professionals and peer support personnel. Mental health professionals serving on a critical incident stress debriefing team possess at least a master's degree in psychology, social work, psychiatric nursing, psychiatry, or mental health counseling. Peer support personnel are trained and prepared to work with mental health professionals in preventing and mitigating the negative impact of acute stress on their fellow workers. All team members receive training in crisis intervention, stress, post-traumatic stress disorder, and the debriefing process.

The following is a brief description of each phase of the debriefing model:

Introductory Phase. During this first phase the leader and team members introduce themselves to the participants. The leader describes how a debriefing works and lists the ground rules for the debriefing. The rules are as follows:

- No one is compelled to talk, but participation is strongly encouraged.
- No notes or recordings of any kind are taken during the debriefing.
- Strict confidentiality is maintained.
- The debriefing is not intended to be therapy.

It is important to convey to participants that their chances for a successful debriefing increase when participants are made fully aware of what to expect during the process.

Fact Phase. The fact phase begins with the team leader asking participants to identify themselves and briefly mention their degree of involvement with the incident. For example, participants may relate their role in the incident, how they were informed of the incident, where they were when they received this news, and so forth. Participants may begin relating their first reactions to the incident. This type of information lays the groundwork for the remaining phases of the process.

Thought Phase. Participants are asked what their first thoughts were concerning the incident. The thought phase begins to personalize the experience for the participants. This is the first phase in which some participants may exhibit some reluctance to share. Participants are asked to discuss "what was the worst part of the event for them, personally." This phase generally causes participants to begin exploring some of their deeper, personal responses to the event. Depending on the intensity of the event and the number of participants, this segment may last thirty minutes to one hour.

Symptom Phase. Participants are asked to describe the signs and symptoms of any distress they experienced, such as feeling nauseated, sweating palms, or having difficulty making decisions. Usually three occurrences of signs and symptoms are discussed: (1) those that appeared at the time of the incident, (2) those that arose during the next few days, and (3) those that they are still experiencing at the time of the debriefing.

Teaching Phase. During the teaching phase the leader and team members share information regarding the relationship between the critical incident and the subsequent cognitive, emotional, behavioral, and physiological reactions that others involved in such events have experienced. Participants are provided with a handout entitled "Critical Stress Information Sheet." During this phase, participants may ask new questions or bring up information that was not discussed earlier.

Re-entry Phase. This phase signals the end of the debriefing. Participants are encouraged to ask questions and explore other issues associated with the incident that may have not surfaced earlier. Team members are asked to provide some summary remarks, and the team leader makes a few additional statements in an effort to bring closure to the debriefing. A crucial message emanating from the debriefing is that the participants' reactions are normal responses to an abnormal event.

The decision about whether or not a formal debriefing is warranted generally rests with management personnel following consultation with mental health consultants. Though not all-inclusive, some examples of important questions to explore when assessing the need for a debriefing are these:

- What is the nature of the incident?
- Is the event of sufficient magnitude as to cause significant emotional distress among those involved?
- How many individuals are affected by the incident?
- What signs and symptoms of distress are being displayed by the witnesses to the incident?
- Are the signs and symptoms growing worse as time passes?
- Are any of the following key indicators of a need for a debriefing present: behavior change; regression; continued symptoms; intensifying symptoms; new symptoms arising; or group symptoms?

In some instances, as these and other questions are explored, it may be determined that a formal debriefing is not warranted. Or, perhaps there may be a decision to briefly meet with the group(s) that have been affected by the incidents to further assess the need for a formal debriefing. Under these circumstances, a critical incident stress defusing may be appropriate.

Management Steps to Help an Organization Recover

- Managers need to spend ample time with their employees, in person at the worksite or wherever they may be. Employees at the worksite need to be reassured about their concerns, and they need to be able to ask questions. Senior management should ensure that immediate supervisors are supported in this role, relieved of unnecessary duties, and not pulled away from their subordinates to write lengthy reports or prepare elaborate briefings.
- Employees will have many questions, and they need the answers—often more than once—if they are to resolve the experience for themselves. Information will develop over time, so information strategies need to be simple and fluid. A notice board at the elevator or a recorded message on a hotline number may suffice for the basics, and a user-friendly system for individual questions needs to be established.
- Union representatives can help in reassuring employees after an incident and in getting information to employees.

- Before an incident ever occurs, the planning group should identify trained mental health professionals in the organization or the community who would be available to respond in the event of an incident. When an incident occurs, involve these emergency mental health consultants as soon as possible. They will generally meet with management first, working down the chain, and then with line employees. Based on what the consultants learn, they will offer services such as debriefings, defusings, and informal counseling, perhaps in the work area.

- The formal debriefing doesn't end the recovery process. Provide opportunities for employees to talk informally with one another when they feel a need to discuss the experience. A comfortable break area and flexibility about break times may be all that is needed.

- Keep work groups together as much as possible, and try not to isolate employees from their normal support groups at work. Show respect and support for employees' efforts to care for one another.

- Initially, the site of a violent incident will be secured as a crime scene. After the authorities are finished with it, management needs to be sensitive to a number of issues. It is helpful if employees don't have to come back to work and face painful reminders such as bloodstains or broken furniture. But on the other hand, the area should not be so "sanitized" that it gives the appearance that management is pretending nothing happened. If someone has died, that person's work area will be a focus of grieving, and it needs to be respected as such.

- Effective coordination with the media and timely dissemination of information can help reduce media pressure on those who are the most vulnerable. Assistance with benefits and other administrative issues can reduce the burden on victims and families.

Following an incident of workplace violence:

- Encourage employees to report and log all incidents and threats of workplace violence.
- Provide prompt medical evaluation and treatment after the incident.
- Report violent incidents to the local police promptly.
- Inform victims of their legal right to prosecute perpetrators.
- Discuss the circumstances of the incident with staff members.
- Encourage employees to share information about ways to avoid similar situations in the future.
- Offer stress debriefing sessions and post-traumatic counseling services to help workers recover from a violent incident.
- Investigate all violent incidents and threats, monitor trends in violent incidents by type or circumstance, and institute corrective actions.
- Discuss changes in the program during regular employee meetings.

- Returning soon, if only briefly, to a feared site can help prevent lasting effects such as phobic responses. Having a friend or loved one along, or being supported by close work associates, may make the first step much easier.
- Getting back to work can be reassuring, and a sense of having a mission to perform can help the group recover its morale. But the return to work must be managed in a way that conveys appropriate respect for the deceased, the injured, and the traumatized.

For further information, see www.opm.gov/employment_and_benefits/worklife/officialdocuments/handbooksguides/WorkplaceViolence/p3-s6.asp.

DEALING WITH THE CONSEQUENCES OF VIOLENCE

Violence may occur in the workplace in spite of preventive measures. Employers should be prepared to deal with the consequences of this violence by providing an environment that promotes open communication and by developing written procedures for reporting and responding to violence. Employers should offer and encourage counseling whenever a worker is threatened or assaulted.

"What Would You Do If" Scenarios

Test out your understanding of violence containment principles in the following scenarios. In each case, think about what you would do prior to reading our suggestions. Feel free to adapt or even challenge our suggestions. You may be able to come up with better responses, particularly as they apply to your environment or personal attributes (e.g., security or law enforcement expertise, martial arts training, gender, size and physical presence, personality, interpersonal skills, etc.).

SCENARIO 1—THE DRUNKEN CONTRACTORS (ALTERNATE VERSION)

Several individuals on a contractor crew drink their lunch. Unlike the version of this scenario in Step 3, however, they are *not* stopped at the employee entrance and they return to work in the machine room. An argument ensues in the area of their job boxes—providing abundant tools as potential weapons.

Suggested Response: Immediately notify security and the police. Secure all entrances to the machine room and clear all adjacent rooms and hallways. Alert health services. Be ready to provide:

1. A description of the machine room and its contents and whether other employees also are in the room.

2. A physical description of the drunken contractors: age, weight, hair color and length, clothing, facial hair, and any other distinguishing features.
3. Observations of their behavior since returning from lunch.

Wait for security and/or police to arrive. Take no precipitous action.

SCENARIO 2—THE TERRORIST

Al Kyda has created an explosive device from materials available at the facility (or smuggled in). Al has taken over the cafeteria, where he is holding about twenty employees hostage.

Suggested Response: Immediately notify security and the police. Secure all entrances to the cafeteria and evacuate the facility. Alert health services. Be ready to provide

1. A description of the cafeteria.
2. A physical description of Al: age, weight, hair color and length, clothing, facial hair, and any other distinguishing features.
3. All information known about Al. If he is an employee, locate his manager and HR representative.

Wait for security and/or police to arrive. Take no precipitous action.

If Al contacts you with demands prior to their arrival, apply the coping guidelines from Step 3 and agree to all his demands where possible and within reason. At a minimum, tell him that you are communicating his demands to those who can make them happen.

Case Studies

The following case studies are taken from the U.S Office of Personal Management and are provided to help you think through similar incidents and determine if your prevention and response plans are adequate. (For these and other case studies, see the U.S. Office of Personnel Management's *Dealing with Workplace Violence*, available at www.opm.gov/employment_and_benefits/worklife/officialdocuments/handbooksguides/workplaceviolence/full.pdf.)

CASE STUDY 1: DOMESTIC VIOLENCE IN THE WORKPLACE

A female employee had broken off a romantic relationship with a male co-worker, but he wouldn't leave her alone. She finally had a restraining order served to him. After receiving the restraining order, the perpetrator lost control and entered the woman's office. He hit her; she fell from her chair. While she was on the floor, he broke a soda bottle and cut her face with the broken glass. While this was going on, coworkers heard the commotion and called the police. The perpetrator fled the scene before police arrived and the victim was transported to the hospital. . . .

The employee remained hospitalized for two days and then went to the home of a friend until the perpetrator was apprehended. She remained at home for another two weeks before returning to work. She continues to stay in touch with the Employee Assistance Program counselor who had visited her at the hospital and assisted her during her time away from the office. The counselor referred her to a support group for battered women, and she finds it very helpful.

Questions for the Planning Group

Who would monitor the proceedings of the criminal case, e.g., to be aware of the situation if the perpetrator got out of jail on bail or probation?

Does your security office maintain liaison with and keep in contact with local law enforcement authorities in order to coordinate efforts in these type of cases?

Do you have a procedure in place for cleaning up the scene of the incident after investigators are finished examining it?

Would employees know whom to call in an emergency such as this?

CASE STUDY 2: THREATENED SUICIDE

A member of the organization's incident response team received a frantic call from an employee saying that her coworker just left her office muttering about "the final straw—you all won't have me to push around any more." The caller said she's been worried for weeks about the possibility of her coworker committing suicide and knows now she should have called earlier. The staff member who took the call told the employee to see if she could find her coworker and remain with her. Help was on its way.

For incidents involving suicide threats, the organization's plan was to call local police if there seemed to be imminent danger and, if not enough was known about the situation, to contact security and the Employee Assistance Program counselor to do an immediate assessment of the situation.

The team member who took the initial call first contacted a security officer, who immediately located the two employees. The EAP counselor could not be reached immediately, so the team member called an employee in the HR department who had earlier volunteered to help out in emergency situations (she had been trained in her community in dealing with suicide attempts).

The HR specialist arrived at the distressed employee's office within two minutes of the call. The employee was crying at this point and making statements such as "No one can help me" and "It'll be over soon." The HR specialist recognized what was happening and asked the security officer to call police and an ambulance and tell them there was a suicide attempt. After calling the police, the security officer went outside to meet the emergency workers and direct them to the scene. The HR specialist then learned from the woman that an hour earlier she had swallowed ten pills. The police and ambulance were on the scene within three minutes of the call and the woman was hospitalized.

The HR specialist contacted the employee's family and then prepared a report of the incident. The counselor consoled and supported the coworker who had initially called the incident response team.

Emergency treatment was successful, and the employee was admitted to the hospital's psychiatric unit. The counselor and HR specialist stayed in touch with the employee and supported her in planning her return to work. She returned to work four weeks later, functioning with the help of antidepressant medication and twice-weekly psychotherapy sessions.

With the employee's consent, the counselor arranged a meeting involving the employee, her supervisor, and the HR specialist to coordinate her treatment and work activities. The supervisor agreed to adjust the employee's work schedule to fit her therapy appointments as a reasonable accommodation, and the supervisor provided guidance on procedures and medical documentation requirements for leave approval. The counselor, supervisor, and employee agreed on a plan for getting the employee immediate emergency help if she should feel another crisis coming on.

Two years later, the employee is doing well, working a normal schedule, and continues to be a productive employee. She no longer takes antidepressant medication, but she stays in touch with both her psychiatrist and the counselor.

Questions for the Planning Group

Do you agree with the organization's approach in this case?

Does your organization have backup plans for situations where key team members are not available?

Has your organization identified employees with skills in handling emergencies?

Does your workplace violence policy and training encourage employees to report incidents at an early stage?

Does your workplace violence policy and training encourage employees to seek guidance with regard to problems that trouble them even when they don't fully understand the nature of the problem?

If the employee had left the building before emergency personnel arrived, does your plan provide for contacting the appropriate authorities?

Risk Assessment Checklist

1. Conventional Security Measures
2. Means to Safely Communicate Dangerous Situation
3. Policies
4. Incident Reporting and Tracking Process
5. An Alternative Reporting Process
6. Clear and Consistent Commitment by Management
7. Hiring Process
8. Discipline, Termination, and Lay-Off Processes
9. Training of Supervisors and Managers
10. Training of Employees
11. Employee Assistance Program
12. Crisis Management Program
13. Periodic Testing of the Systems and Processes
14. Ongoing Reviews and Assessments of the Program

1. Conventional Security Measures

ASSESSMENT OF CURRENT SITUATION

- Does each facility have security guards in place—in the lobby and patrolling the corridors and offices? Uniformed? Employee or contractor?
- Are the guards effective? Or disruptive and inhibiting—and a potential source of violence?
- Is there a drop-down gate in place at lobby entrances?
- Is it possible to access the facility without going through the lobby?
- Are all employees issued photo and/or electronic security IDs? Are they inspected at entrance?
- Do visitors sign in and sign out? Are they issued temporary (date-stamped) IDs?
- Are all packages, briefcases, and pocketbooks inspected at entrance?
- Are metal detectors in place at all entrances?
- Are security cameras in place? At all key locations? Are they regularly monitored?
- Is there an electronic alarm system? At all points of access? What happens when triggered?
- Is the layout of building optimum for safety (e.g., wide hallways, large rooms)?
- Are there a large number of outsiders and a high outsider-to-staff ratio?
- Is there sufficient lighting in the parking lot?
- Do all of your employees *feel* safe?

SELF-INSPECTION SECURITY CHECKLIST

Facility: _____

Inspector: _____

Date of Inspection: _____

1. **Security Control Plan** ___ yes ___ no
   If yes, does it contain:
   (A) Policy Statement ___ yes ___ no
   (B) Review of Employee Incident Exposure ___ yes ___ no
   (C) Methods of Control ___ yes ___ no
       If yes, does it include:
         Engineering ___ yes ___ no
         Work Practice ___ yes ___ no
         Training ___ yes ___ no
         Reporting Procedures ___ yes ___ no
         Recordkeeping ___ yes ___ no
         Counseling ___ yes ___ no
   (D) Evaluation of Incidents ___ yes ___ no
   (E) Floor Plan ___ yes ___ no
   (F) Protection of Assets ___ yes ___ no
   (G) Computer Security ___ yes ___ no
   (H) Plan Accessible to All Employees ___ yes ___ no
   (I) Plan Reviewed and Updated Annually ___ yes ___ no
   (J) Plan Reviewed and Updated When Tasks Added or Changed ___ yes ___ no

2. **Policy Statement by Employer** ___ yes ___ no

3. **Work Areas Evaluated by Employer** ___ yes ___ no
   If yes, how often? _____

4. **Engineering Controls** ___ yes ___ no
   If yes, does it include:
   (A) Mirrors to see around corners and in blind spots ___ yes ___ no
   (B) Landscaping to provide unobstructed view of the workplace ___ yes ___ no
   (C) "Fishbowl effect" to allow unobstructed view of the interior ___ yes ___ no
   (D) Limiting the posting of sale signs on windows ___ yes ___ no
   (E) Adequate lighting in and around the workplace ___ yes ___ no
   (F) Parking lot well lighted ___ yes ___ no
   (G) Door Control(s) ___ yes ___ no
   (H) Panic Button(s) ___ yes ___ no
   (I) Door Detector(s) ___ yes ___ no
   (J) Closed-Circuit TV ___ yes ___ no
   (K) Stationary Metal Detector ___ yes ___ no
   (L) Sound Detection ___ yes ___ no
   (M) Intrusion Detection System ___ yes ___ no
   (N) Intrusion Panel ___ yes ___ no
   (O) Monitor(s) ___ yes ___ no

(P) Videotape Recorder ___ yes ___ no
(Q) Switcher ___ yes ___ no
(R) Handheld Metal Detector ___ yes ___ no
(S) Handheld Video Camera ___ yes ___ no
(T) Personnel Traps ("Sally traps") ___ yes ___ no
(U) Other _____ ___ yes ___ no

5. **Structural Modifications**
   Plexiglas, Glass Guard, Wire Glass, Partitions, etc. ___ yes ___ no
   If yes, comment: _____

6. **Security Guards** ___ yes ___ no
   (A) If yes, are there an appropriate number for the site? ___ yes ___ no
   (B) Are they knowledgeable of the company ___ yes ___ no
        workplace violence prevention policy?
   (C) Indicate if they are:
        _____ Contract Guards
        _____ In-House Employees
   (D) At Entrance(s) ___ yes ___ no
   (E) Building Patrol ___ yes ___ no
   (F) Guards provided with communication? ___ yes ___ no
        If yes, indicate what type: _____
   (G) Guards receive training on workplace violence ___ yes ___ no
        situations?
   Comments: _____

7. **Work Practice Controls** ___ yes ___ no
   If yes, indicate:
   (A) Desks Clear of Objects That May Become Missiles ___ yes ___ no
   (B) Unobstructed Office Exits ___ yes ___ no
   (C) Vacant (Bare) Cubicles Available ___ yes ___ no
   (D) Reception Area Available ___ yes ___ no
   (E) Visitor/Client Sign In/Out ___ yes ___ no
   (F) Visitor(s)/Client(s) Escorted ___ yes ___ no
   (G) Barriers to Separate Clients from Work Area ___ yes ___ no
   (H) One Entrance Used ___ yes ___ no
   (I) Separate Interview Area(s) ___ yes ___ no
   (J) ID Badges Used ___ yes ___ no
   (K) Emergency Numbers Posted by Phones ___ yes ___ no
   (L) Internal Phone System ___ yes ___ no
        If yes, indicate:
        Does it use 120 VAC building lines? ___ yes ___ no
        Does it use phone lines? ___ yes ___ no
   (M) Internal Procedures for Conflict (Problem) Situations ___ yes ___ no
   (N) Procedures for Employee Dismissal ___ yes ___ no
   (O) Limit Spouse and Family Visits to Designated Areas ___ yes ___ no
   (P) Key Control Procedures ___ yes ___ no
   (Q) Access Control to the Workplace ___ yes ___ no
   (R) Objects That May Become Missiles Removed from ___ yes ___ no
        Area

(S)   Parking Prohibited in Fire Zones   ___ yes ___ no
Other: _____

7a. Off-Premises Work Practice Controls
(For staff who work away from a fixed workplace, such as social services, real estate, utilities, policy/fire/sanitation, taxi/limo, construction, sales/delivery, messengers, and others)

		yes	no
(A)	Trained in Hazardous Situation Avoidance	___	___
(B)	Briefed about Areas Where They Work	___	___
(C)	Have Reviewed Past Incidents by Type and Area	___	___
(D)	Know Directions and Routes for Day's Schedule	___	___
(E)	Previewed Client/Case Histories	___	___
(F)	Left an Itinerary with Contact Information	___	___
(G)	Have Periodic Check-In Procedures	___	___
(H)	After-Hours Contact Procedures	___	___
(I)	Partnering Arrangements If Deemed Necessary	___	___
(J)	Know How to Control/Defuse Potentially Violent Situations	___	___
(K)	Supplied with Personal Alarm/Cell Phone/Radio	___	___
(L)	Limit Visible Clues of Carrying Money/Valuables	___	___
(M)	Carry Forms to Record Incidents by Area	___	___
(N)	Know Procedures if Involved in Incident	___	___

8. Training Conducted   ___ yes ___ no
If yes, is it:
(A)   Prior to Initial Assignment   ___ yes ___ no
(B)   At Least Annually Thereafter   ___ yes ___ no
(C)   Does It Include:

	yes	no
Components of Security Control Plan	___	___
Engineering and Workplace Controls Instituted at Workplace	___	___
Techniques to Use in Potentially Volatile Situations	___	___
How to Anticipate/Read Behavior	___	___
Procedures to Follow after an Incident	___	___
Periodic Refresher for On-Site Procedures	___	___
Recognizing Abuse/Paraphernalia	___	___
Opportunity for Q and A with Instructor	___	___
Hazards Unique to Job Tasks	___	___

9. Written Training Records Kept   ___ yes ___ no

10. Are Incidents Reported   ___ yes ___ no
If yes, are they:
(A)   Reported in Written Form   ___ yes ___ no
(B)   First Report of Injury Form (If Employee Loses Time)   ___ yes ___ no

11. Incidents Evaluated   ___ yes ___ no
(A)   EAP Counseling Offered   ___ yes ___ no

(B) Other Action (Reporting Requirements, Suggestions, Reporting to Local Authorities, etc.): _____

(C) Are Steps Taken to Prevent Recurrence?   ___ yes ___ no

12. **Floor Plans Posted Showing Exits, Entrances, Location of Security Equipment, Etc.**   ___ yes ___ no
If yes, does it:
(A) Include an Emergency Action Plan, Evacuation   ___ yes ___ no
Plan, and/or a Disaster Contingency Plan?

13. **Do Employees Feel Safe?**   ___ yes ___ no
(A) Have employees been surveyed to find out their   ___ yes ___ no
concerns?
(B) Has the employer utilized the crime prevention   ___ yes ___ no
services and/or lectures provided by the local or
state police?
Comments: _____
General Comments/Recommendations: _____

- Is there an appropriate balance between *safety/security* considerations and *budget*; *access* and *comfort* for employees and customers; and the organization's *mission*?

RECOMMENDATIONS _____

2. Means to Safely Communicate Dangerous Situation

ASSESSMENT OF CURRENT SITUATION:

- Is there an established duress alarm system (electronic or procedural) for alerting others on staff and the police?
- A silent, out-of-sight way to signal others (security, management, police)?
- An intercom or PA system and coded messages, e.g., "Paging Mr. Strong"?
- An innocuous code for an employee to use, which alerts a coworker in the vicinity to get help, e.g., "Oh, Bob, would you let Mr. Strong know that he needs to check his messages"?
- Do all employees know of and know how to use the systems/procedures?
- Upon becoming aware of a dangerous situation, does each person on staff know:
  - Whom they are to notify (and how)?
  - Who will perform what task upon being notified?
  - How to protect themselves, coworkers, and customers?

RECOMMENDATIONS _____

3. Policies

The policies should clearly state the organization's stand on violent, disruptive and threatening behavior, as well as weapons in the workplace.

ASSESSMENT OF CURRENT SITUATION:

- Does your policy clearly state this?
- When was the last time it was communicated? How? Issued by a senior executive?
- Is it posted at entrances, employment office, and break areas?
- Is it included in the employee handbook?
- Is it verbally communicated during new employee orientation, in department meetings, and in training sessions?
- Are there any unkept promises or unenforced provisions in the policy?
- Does your harassment policy cover *all* forms of harassment, intimidation and violence?

RECOMMENDATIONS _____

4. Incident Reporting and Tracking Process

This process allows you to identify trends and vulnerabilities that may not otherwise be obvious.

ASSESSMENT OF CURRENT SITUATION:

- Is there such a process in place? Is there an appropriate form for it?
- Does it include workplace violence, verbal abuse, emotional outbursts, or threats (rather than focused just on physical accidents, injuries, and illnesses)?
- Who completes the report? (For example, all managers, just safety/HR?) Are they trained in how to do it?
- Who tracks the reports and monitors trends/vulnerabilities? To whom are the results reported?
- Do all employees know of it and feel comfortable using it?
- Is the process integrated with:
  ○ Workplace violence policy, reporting requirements, and training
  ○ Sexual harassment policy, reporting requirements, and training
  ○ Safety policy, reporting requirements, and training

RECOMMENDATIONS _____

5. An Alternative Reporting Process

This is needed in case the conventional channels and chains of command fail or aren't trusted.

ASSESSMENT OF CURRENT SITUATION:

- Is there such an alternative process?
- Is it included in the relevant policies? Has it been clearly communicated and reiterated?
- Is there an ombudsman-type of manager (preferably more than one)—or an internal or external hotline—with confidentiality safeguards?
- Are the specified people/titles perceived by most employees as approachable?
- Do they represent as much diversity as possible?
- Is "strange" behavior or disrespect regarded as appropriate to report?

RECOMMENDATIONS _____

6. Clear and Consistent Commitment by Management

Management should be committed to a safe workplace—and to a culture of civility and respect.

ASSESSMENT OF CURRENT SITUATION:

- Is there a safety policy? Has it been effectively communicated?
- Is there a safety committee? Is it active—e.g., meeting regularly?
- Do they deal with interpersonal threats (or just physical/environmental hazards)?
- Is there a clear commitment to a culture of civility and respect (e.g., in the mission statement)?
- Has this commitment been communicated in writing and verbally (e.g., during new employee orientation, in department meetings, and in training sessions)?
- Is there an equal concern for employees as for customers? Are they treated as important ends in themselves?
- Do schisms (involving isolation, hostility, or resentment) exist? (For example, between administration and operations, support staff and managers, younger/newer and older/long-service staff members—or between facilities, departments, genders, races, and/or different personalities.)
- Have managers been trained in motivation and feedback skills?

- Have employees received safety training?
- Have employees received training in interpersonal skills and teamwork?

RECOMMENDATIONS _____

7. Hiring Process

A hiring process that screens out the potentially violent or unstable is an organization's first line of defense.

ASSESSMENT OF CURRENT SITUATION:

- Does the HR function participate in and control *all* hiring?
- Are applications and resumes reviewed for *behavioral problems* (not just skills)? By HR?
- Gaps in employment/education history, job-hopping, etc.?
- Anything suspicious or inconsistent?
- Are *broad* background checks conducted (not just criminal record checks)? For *all* jobs?
- Are prior employers (i.e., actual *supervisors*) contacted? By trained HR staff? For *all* jobs?
- Are character/behavior-related issues (not just dates of employment or skills) probed?
- Is drug testing conducted? For *all* jobs?
- Is validated psychological testing conducted? For *all* jobs?
- Does HR conduct an in-depth interview (looking for behavioral problems) of all candidates prior to job offer?
  - "Behavioral interview" questions, e.g., "Give an example of how you performed under stress"?
  - Careful probing of reason for leaving/actual supervisor/title/responsibilities/dates?
- Are restrictions placed on the process (e.g., by union contracts or a misunderstanding of EEO/labor laws) preventing the potentially violent or unstable from being screened out?
- Are contract/temporary workers effectively screened?
- Have supervisors and HR staff received training in interviewing and screening?

RECOMMENDATIONS _____

8. Discipline, Termination, and Lay-Off Processes

❑ Preserve the involved employees' dignity
❑ Include the tactful and safe handling of high-risk employees and situations
❑ Handled by an objective third party such as HR

ASSESSMENT OF CURRENT SITUATION:

- Are there pre-discipline and pre-termination approval processes (involving HR)?
- Is there an established process for the termination itself?
- Do these processes preserve the employee's dignity?
- Is the termination itself conducted by HR (i.e., "objective third party")?
- Are all discipline and termination communications conducted by management and/or HR (rather than support staff)?
- Are there restrictions (e.g., by corporate culture, union contracts, or a misunderstanding of EEO/labor laws) preventing discipline or termination of problem employees?
- Is there is a mutually clear process for disciplining or terminating a contract employee?
- Is there a reluctance to discipline/terminate employees (including contract employees) who are marginal performers?
- Are the standards of acceptable performance and behavior (including contractors) high enough?
- Have supervisors and HR staff receiving training in discipline and termination?

RECOMMENDATIONS

9. Training of Supervisors and Managers

❑ Proper discipline and terminations
❑ The warning signs of a dangerous employee, and the triggering events
❑ Their duty to report—not just overt violence and threats
❑ How to de-escalate dangerous situations
❑ Their role in response and crisis management
❑ Their responsibility to treat all people with respect and dignity
❑ How to detect the behavioral "profile" during interviews and reference checks

ASSESSMENT OF CURRENT SITUATION:

- Have supervisors, managers and HR staff received training in all of the above?
- Have they received training in
  - Behavioral interviewing skills?
  - How to safely terminate an individual, maintaining his or her dignity and respect?
  - Effective people management—motivating employees, providing feedback, performance coaching, listening skills?

RECOMMENDATIONS _____

10. Training of Employees

❑ Workplace violence awareness and reporting processes
❑ Interpersonal skills, e.g., attitude, assertion, listening, anger management
❑ Teamwork

ASSESSMENT OF CURRENT SITUATION:

- Do employees know they should report violent acts and _warning signs_?
- Do they know what to look for?
- Do they know how to defuse or de-escalate a potentially violent person?
- Do they know how to protect themselves and coworkers when threatened?
- What is the level of employees' interpersonal and teamwork skills?

RECOMMENDATIONS:

- Conduct workplace violence awareness training for all employees addressing:
  - The nature and scope of workplace violence
  - The warning signs and triggering events of violence
  - How to defuse or de-escalate a potentially violent person
  - How to protect yourself and coworkers when threatened
- Offer interpersonal skills training for employees.
- Offer teamwork skills training for employees.
- Hold team-building events for the entire staff.

11. Employee Assistance Program

❑ To aid the troubled employee _before_ he or she becomes threatening or violent
❑ To act as a beneficial partner _following_ an incident

ASSESSMENT OF CURRENT SITUATION:

- Is there a contract with an EAP? What is the quality of the program?
- Are employees encouraged to utilize the services of the EAP?
- To what extent is EAP referral considered for troubled employees who are not yet violent or substance abusing?

RECOMMENDATIONS _____

12. Crisis Management Program

Putting in place a detailed, well-rehearsed program can minimize

- ❏ Injury, damage, and disruption
- ❏ Confusion, panic, and fear
- ❏ Blame casting, including self-blame
- ❏ A sense of victimization

ASSESSMENT OF CURRENT SITUATION:

- Is there an established crisis management program? Does it address workplace violence?
- Does it include detailed procedures specifying *who* does *what* and *when*? For example:
  - ° How to restrain the perpetrator (if appropriate)
  - ° Dealing with the perpetrator after the incident
  - ° How to contain the incident and evacuation protocols
  - ° Notification of security staff and/or police
  - ° Summoning of medical staff
  - ° Communications—during the incident and afterward
  - ° Providing EAP support
- Do all relevant parties know their roles?
- Is it well rehearsed, e.g., with drills?

RECOMMENDATIONS _____

13. Periodic Testing of the Systems and Processes

ASSESSMENT OF CURRENT SITUATION:

- Have all the foregoing systems and procedures been tested, e.g., with drills?
- With what results?
- What modifications/improvements can and should be made?

RECOMMENDATIONS _____

14. Ongoing Reviews and Assessments of the Program

ASSESSMENT OF CURRENT SITUATION:

- Are reviews and assessments conducted periodically, and after every incident?
- Who is responsible for such reviews? To whom are the assessments communicated?
- Are appropriate modifications made in light of the assessments?

RECOMMENDATIONS _____

Incident Report Form

1. VICTIM'S NAME: _____
   Job Title: _____

2. VICTIM'S ADDRESS: _____
   _____

3. HOME PHONE NUMBER: _____
   WORK PHONE NUMBER: _____

4. EMPLOYER'S NAME AND ADDRESS: _____
   _____

5. DEPARTMENT/SECTION: _____

6. VICTIM'S SOCIAL SECURITY NUMBER: _____

7. INCIDENT DATE: _____

8. INCIDENT TIME: _____

9. INCIDENT LOCATION: _____

10. WORK LOCATION (if different): _____

11. TYPE OF INCIDENT (circle one):
    Assault, Robbery, Harassment, Disorderly Conduct, Sex Offense, Other
    (please specify)_____

12. WERE YOU INJURED?   ___ yes ___ no
    If yes, please specify your injuries and the location of any treatment:
    _____
    _____

13. DID POLICE RESPOND TO INCIDENT?   ___ yes ___ no

14. WHAT POLICE DEPARTMENT? _____

15. POLICE REPORT FILED?   ___ yes ___ no
    REPORT NUMBER: _____

16. WAS YOUR SUPERVISOR NOTIFIED?   ___ yes ___ no

17. SUPERVISOR'S NAME: _____

18. WAS THE LOCAL UNION/EMPLOYEE   ___ yes ___ no
    REPRESENTATIVENOTIFIED?
    Who should be notified: _____

19. WAS ANY ACTION TAKEN BY EMPLOYER? (specify)
    _____

20. ASSAILANT/PERPETRATOR (circle one):
    Intruder, Customer, Patient, Resident, Client, Visitor, Student, Coworker,
    Former Employee, Supervisor, Family/Friend, Other (specify) _____

21. ASSAILANT/PERPETRATOR—NAME/ADDRESS/AGE (if known):
    _____

22. PLEASE BRIEFLY DESCRIBE THE INCIDENT:
    _____

_____

_____

23. INCIDENT DISPOSITION (circle all that apply):
No action taken, Arrest, Warning, Suspension, Reprimand, Other: _____
24. DID THE INCIDENT INVOLVE A WEAPON?   ___ yes   ___ no
If yes, specify:_____
25. DID YOU LOSE ANY WORK DAYS?   ___ yes   ___ no
Specify: _____
26. WERE YOU SINGLED OUT OR WAS THE VIOLENCE DIRECTED AT
MORE THAN ONE INDIVIDUAL?_____
27. WERE YOU ALONE WHEN THE INCIDENT OCCURRED?_____
28. DID YOU HAVE ANY REASON TO BELIEVE THAT AN   ___ yes   ___ no
INCIDENT MIGHT OCCUR?
Why? _____
29. HAS THIS TYPE OR SIMILAR INCIDENT(S)   ___ yes   ___ no
HAPPENED TO YOU OR YOUR COWORKERS?
If yes, specify:_____
30. HAVE YOU HAD ANY COUNSELING OR SUPPORT   ___ yes   ___ no
SINCE THE INCIDENT?
If yes, specify:_____
31. WHAT DO YOU FEEL CAN BE DONE IN THE FUTURE TO AVOID
SUCH AN INCIDENT?

_____

32. WAS THIS ASSAILANT INVOLVED IN PREVIOUS   ___ yes   ___ no
INCIDENTS?
If so, specify:_____
33. ARE THERE ANY MEASURES IN PLACE TO PREVENT   ___ yes   ___ no
SIMILAR INCIDENTS?
If yes, specify:_____
34. HAS CORRECTIVE ACTION BEEN TAKEN?   ___ yes   ___ no
If yes, specify:_____
35. OTHER COMMENTS:

_____

_____

_____

Bomb Threat Check Sheet

Be calm. Be courteous. Listen. Do not interrupt the caller.
If possible, get the attention of other personnel by a signal or note.

THE CALL:
Date/Time: _____ Caller ID: _____ Received on line: _____

CALLER'S SEX: MALE/FEMALE   **AGE**: YOUNG/MIDDLE-AGED/OLD

CALLER'S EXACT WORDS:

_____

_____

_____

_____

_____

Keep the caller on the line as long as possible.
Ask to have the message repeated.
Try to get the answer to these questions:

1. When is the bomb going to explode? _____
2. Where is the bomb? _____
3. What does it look like? _____
4. What kind of bomb is it?_____
5. What will cause it to explode? _____
6. Did you place the bomb? Why? _____
7. Where are you calling from?_____
8. What is your name and address?_____

TIME CALLER HUNG UP: _____

CALLER'S VOICE (circle all that apply):

Voice: Load, Soft, Deep, Raspy, Familiar, Pleasant, High-pitched
Accent: Black, British, Southern, European, Hispanic, Asian, Aboriginal, French, Other
Speech: Fast, Slow, Lisp, Nasal, Slurred, Stutter, Distinct, Intoxicated, Impediment
Manner: Calm, Angry, Excited, Rational, Irrational, Coherent, Incoherent, Laughter, Righteous
Language: Foul, Poor, Fluent, Broken, Emotional, Repeating, Excellent, Reading Statement

BACKGROUND NOISE (circle all that apply):

Music, Trains, PA system, Quiet, Voices, Telephones, Party, Animals, Mixed, Street traffic, Aircraft, Bedlam, Children, Office machines, Factory machines

OTHER: _____

CALL RECEIVED BY: _____

CALL SECURITY IMMEDIATELY @ XXX-XXXX.

STEP FIVE

Prevent

As with most other risks, prevention of workplace violence begins with planning. As with other risks, it is easier to persuade managers to focus on the problem after a violent act has taken place than it is to get them to act before anything has happened. If the decision to plan in advance is more difficult to make, however, it is also more logical.

Any organization, large or small, will be far better able to spot potential dangers and threats and defuse them before violence develops and will be able to manage a crisis better if one does occur, if its executives have considered the issue beforehand and have prepared policies, practices, and structures to deal with it.

Open communication is the essential first step to preventing violence in the workplace. Employees do not become violent overnight; there are warning signs. Recognizing these signs can be the difference between life and death. Employers must enforce a policy that violence, intimidation, verbal abuse, and harassment will not be tolerated.

Managers need to know their employees. Effectively using open communication, active listening, and direct observation can reduce the risk of office violence. Recommending that an employee seek professional assistance is an integral part of good human resource/personnel management and a positive method to prevent potential violence in the workplace.

Training should educate supervisors and workers to identify violence in its various forms, catch the warning signs that an individual could potentially turn violent, and become sensitive to the consequences of disregarding violent and threatening signs and actions. Prevention is the key. Employees should be encouraged to use their chain of command to report individuals in their work areas who have shown the warning signs of potentially turning violent.

10 Keys to Prevent Violence from Scarring Your Workplace

1. Ensure a Culture of Respect.
2. Reduce Workplace Stress.
3. Establish Violence and Weapons Policies.
4. Use Proper Employee-Selection Techniques.
5. Standardize Discipline and Termination Procedures.
6. Recognize Signs of Trouble, and Ensure They Are Reported.
7. Investigate All Threats, Complaints, and Red Flags.
8. Take Appropriate Action.
9. Train Managers, Employees, and Security Personnel.
10. Conduct a Risk Assessment.

1. Ensure a Culture of Respect

In Step 1, we described the organizational factors that can breed workplace violence. The single most important ingredient to prevent your workplace from becoming such a breeding ground is to ensure a culture of respect.

All too often, organizations have viewed their employees in much the same way as they view their material resources: as a commodity, homogeneous and easily interchangeable. For example, notice the frequent use of such terms as "human capital," "subordinate," "rank and file," and "headcount"—terms that connote property, servitude, or thing-ness.

In fact, however, employees are not "headcount" or merely the means to organizational ends. They also are ends in themselves. As a *human* resource, an employee deserves (and needs) to be viewed differently than the inanimate resources of the organization. A human being needs to be treated with: *respect*.

The master key to ensuring that your workplace is not a breeding ground for violence—and to tap its full potential—is grasping that fact, not only intellectually, but also in your gut, so that it influences every aspect of how you think about and interact with your fellow employees.

RESPECT

Most of us, perhaps, share a similar understanding of the word *respect*. But the concept is so important that we are elaborating on it.

The American Heritage Dictionary of the English Language defines *respect* as "the state of being regarded with honor or esteem." As a verb, the definition includes "to avoid violation of."

We think that second definition provides an important clarification. By *respect*, we do not mean deference to authority or position (e.g., bowing to a king or "Yessir, boss!"). Rather we mean the American principle of avoiding violation of an individual's fundamental rights. Every human being is a Sir or Ma'am, even when addressing them on an informal, first-name basis.

And we've created an acronym based on the word, which enumerates some of the behaviors associated with it:

Refrain from putdowns, criticism, personal attacks.
Encourage others to state their views.
Support each other—even if you don't agree.
Practice active listening.
Express yourself assertively, not aggressively or submissively.
Collaborate—not compete or collude.
Trust each other . . . unless and until such trust is violated.

In our workshops, we ask participants to commit to these behaviors. We urge you to do likewise in your workplace, and to provide training programs for your employees in the skills entailed.

This employer has come up with an interesting way to ensure that all their employees are treated with respect:

> At Beth Israel Hospital in Boston, doctors occasionally dress as maintenance staff and roam the hospital halls. Why do they do that? To learn how it feels to be treated as "support staff" and to find ways of improving the hospital environment. (Bob Nelson, *1001 Ways to Reward Employees*)

Show your employees that you care about them as persons, not just as workers. For example:

> Publix Super Markets publishes a biweekly bulletin—listing the births, deaths, marriages, and illnesses of employees and their families. For more than 20 years, the president sent personalized cards to the families of everyone in the bulletin. (Bob Nelson, *1001 Ways to Reward Employees*)

By the way, Publix is considered one of the 100 best companies to work for. An important component of workplace respect is sensitivity to and support of the needs and aspirations of your employees.

What do you think employees most want from their jobs? Good wages? Job security? That's what most managers have thought, for at least the past sixty years. But it's not what employees have continued to say. What employees really want is *appreciation* and *involvement*.

Are we saying that wages are unimportant? Of course not. Competitive (and fair) pay and benefits usually are a necessary but not sufficient condition to ensure employee satisfaction.

APPRECIATION

Employees want to be appreciated for the work they do. Praise their accomplishments using *positive feedback*. Here's how to do it:

1. Start by describing the *behavior* (not the person), using specific language and examples. (Over the years, as we've coached managers on feedback, lack of specificity is the major weakness we've observed.)
2. Then describe the *impact* of the behavior: what positive consequences it has, and why you're praising the person for it.
3. And show *appreciation* for the person's effort. This can be as simple as saying: "Thanks!"

Praise not only accomplishments, but also good attempts—just as you would if you were training a puppy or a young child. (No, we are not saying that employees are pets or children, but the principle applies to any living organism.)

And praise accomplishments both large and small. Here's an example of a small reward for a large accomplishment:

> A Hewlett-Packard engineer burst into his manager's office to announce he'd just found the solution to a problem the group had been struggling with for many weeks. His manager quickly groped around his desk for some item to acknowledge the accomplishment and ended up handing the employee a banana from his lunch with the words, "Well done. Congratulations!" The employee was initially puzzled, but over time, the Golden Banana Award became one of the most prestigious honors bestowed on an inventive employee. (Bob Nelson, *1001 Ways to Reward Employees*)

A reward can have little or no monetary value and still be effective. It's the meaning attached to the reward that counts.

Praise at least four times more than you criticize—which, for many of us, is in the reverse proportion to what we tend to receive.

Offer praise promptly, as soon as observed. Praise delayed is praise denied. Don't wait for the annual performance review. Remember the puppy/child principle.

Do it verbally and in writing. And putting it in writing does not have to be time consuming. For example, use your business cards. When you catch someone doing something right, briefly note what they did and how you feel about it. Sign it and hand them the card.

Do it publicly and in private—based on both the magnitude of the accomplishment and the personal preferences of the recipient. Not everyone is comfortable with public praise.

In fact, never criticize or reprimand. Short of illegal or clearly immoral acts, none of us deserves to be reprimanded. Instead, what we deserve and need is to be redirected toward different, more effective behavior. You can accomplish this with *constructive feedback*. Here's how to do it:

1. First, describe the specific, observable *behavior*, using facts—just like positive feedback. Vague generalities and unsubstantiated opinions are useless in improving performance. Avoid judgments and evaluations. Describe the behavior, not the person. This is not a character assessment and certainly not a character assassination.
2. Next, describe the *impact* of the behavior and why you're bringing it to the employee's attention—just like in positive feedback, but this time the impact is undesirable or short of optimum.
3. Then check for the individual's understanding of your feedback and ask for input—*inquiry*. This step is unique to constructive feedback. It's usually not needed in positive feedback. (We say more about how to do this below.)
4. Finally, suggest an alternative by describing the desired behavior—that is, your *expectation*—which takes the place of the appreciation that you expressed in positive feedback.

In practice, you may very well go back and forth between these last two steps—continually checking for understanding and eliciting the employee's ideas, as you talk about the desired behavior.

And do it sincerely. Your goal should be to catch employees doing something right and make them aware of it, not to get them to work harder (although they probably will).

INVOLVEMENT

Involve employees in plans and decisions, especially those that affect them. Elicit their ideas and opinions.

The Dilbert cartoons are known for their humorous commentary on the dysfunctional workplace. An ongoing theme of the series is plans and decisions handed down from on high—in which the employees had no input and which (unsurprisingly) are impossible to implement. Employees want to feel in on things. Do yours? They can, if you elicit their ideas and opinions, using the *inquiry* and *listening* skills.

INQUIRY

What is inquiry? It's the opposite of telling or advocating. You ask for a person's ideas or input in a nonjudgmental way. By tone of voice and reputation, the other person needs to be assured that whatever ideas or opinions he or she expresses will be OK.

You withhold telling what you think and avoid arguing your own point of view—very difficult for many of us! You just inquire . . . and then listen to what the person has to say. Inquiry really is very simple, although not necessarily easy. You merely ask: "What do you think?"

How do you do it? Whenever you face a problem or task, ask for input from the persons involved. Ask what they think should be done. If necessary, get them to open up by probing their prior experiences and perspectives.

So what do you do if their ideas are not workable? Look for parts of the idea to build on or, at a minimum, credit the person for the idea and explain why you can't use it.

ACTIVE LISTENING

Inquiry and listening go hand in hand. If you don't really listen to what the other person has to say in response to your inquiry, you deny yourself and the other person of all the potential positive outcomes. And really listening is not a passive process. You need to actively engage with the other person. There are six elements in active listening (originally described in Step 3 as a component of defusing a hostile person):

1. Stop what you are doing and give the person your full attention.
2. Use silence—and don't complete the other person's sentences.
3. Collect the facts on the issue at hand.
4. Then go deeper. Listen to what is really being said. What does he or she want you to understand?
5. Use reflective questioning—paraphrase/restate comments to get confirmation. "Let me see if I understand you. Are you saying . . . ?" "You want . . . . Is that right?"
6. Ask clarifying and open-ended questions to inquire: "Give me an example." "What would you like to see happen?" "Anything else?" "Tell me more."

If what the other person is saying is very simple and has little emotional content, you may need to apply only the first two elements—i.e., shut up and listen.

Adding a reflective question at the end is always a good idea. For example: "You need to leave work a half-hour early today for personal business and will make up that time by coming in a half-hour early tomorrow. Right? OK!"

However, for anything more complex—and especially if there are emotions involved (e.g., as in a complaint or personal problem or when defusing a hostile person)—you'll definitely want to apply all six elements.

2. Reduce Workplace Stress

In Step 1, we described the negative impact that job demands, burnout, and stress can have both on productivity and on workplace violence. The Families and Work Institute has identified the following types of job demands:

- hours worked
- bringing work home
- nights away from home
- overtime with no notice
- shift work
- job pressures

Most of these have increased in recent years. This is *not* good news—for employee well-being, productivity, or workplace safety. So what to do?

WHAT THE EMPLOYER CAN DO

You can start by doing whatever you can to limit those job demands. Be sure to include job burnout in your equation, when assessing the relative merits of cost-cutting or productivity improvement initiatives. Think about what you can do to limit each type of job demand:

- Discourage excessively long hours and bringing work home, whenever possible.
- Minimize nights away from home (e.g., with virtual meetings).
- Limit overtime (which is a good way to cut costs), and plan for it in advance.
- Accommodate personal preferences in shift assignments, whenever possible.
- Make sure that your productivity expectations are reasonable.
- Use motivation (rather than pressure) to encourage your employees to meet those expectations.

And there is some good news! The Families and Work Institute also found that workplace support appears to buffer or protect employees from the negative effects of job demands. So beef up your workplace support. Here are some examples.

1. Make work more meaningful by applying your organization's core competencies in creative ways.

Try to identify a synergy between your products and services and your employees' values—home, family, recreation, education, giving back to the community, and so forth. For example, Motorola uses its own senior technical staff to conduct in-house technical training courses, some of which are part of accredited MS degree programs. A construction company could provide home repairs for employees. What expertise does your organization have that could be made available to enhance your employees' personal or professional lives? Some hotels allow their employees' children to watch TV in an unrented room while the parent is working. Could you do anything like this at your workplace? For example, perhaps you could utilize available space and employees to provide ad hoc child care during school holidays. And, when disaster strikes, offer your products and services—and volunteers from your workforce—to provide aid.

2. Link the mission and the job to the talents and aspirations of each employee.

In *The Truth about Burnout* (Jossey-Bass, 1997), Maslach and Leiter determined that one of the main causes of burnout is job mismatch (or culture misfit). The characteristics of the job aren't a good match for the employee's talents. Or the perceived purpose and values of the employer clash with those of the employee.

Make hiring and promotion decisions based on:

- Relevant talent (i.e., basic abilities, aptitudes, and inclinations), more than on skills or experience. The need for specific skills changes rapidly—and talented employees can acquire skills and experience.
- Culture fit. And no, we are not talking about superficial attributes like race, gender, age, and so on. Rather, we are talking about the more significant and relevant attribute of values.
- Temperament and lifestyle—if and as relevant to the position. For example, don't expect an introvert to be happy or successful as a telemarketer. And a job requiring extensive travel or weekend work may not be suitable for an individual with parental obligations. (Warning: Don't make assumptions. Instead, ensure that the individual is crystal clear about the job requirements.)

Cascade your organization's mission: Articulate it with increasing and relevant detail for each organizational unit. Flesh it out with goals and action plans for every individual manager and employee, goals and actions that also consider their unique abilities and ambitions.

Do all of this for your entire workforce—part-timers, temps, and contractors, as well. These days, more and more of your workforce are other than regular, full-time. Far too often these others feel left out and treated as second-class citizens.

3. Ensure that each employee has sufficient autonomy to deal with the challenges they face in their jobs.

As Cindy Ventrice, author of *Make Their Day!*, observes:

> Difficult challenges—coupled with a lack of control—create frustration, job burnout, poor performance and turnover. But those very same challenges—when coupled with the ability to make meaningful changes—create enthusiasm, peak performance and loyalty.

Most employees want to do a good job. But when they're frustrated by too many rules, red tape, or micromanaging supervisors—their spirits plunge, their performance suffers, and the best among them look for other opportunities.

Notice the threefold benefit resulting from this example of increased autonomy reported by Bob Nelson in his *1001 Ways to Energize Employees*:

> Nurses at San Diego's Scripps Mercy Hospital have been given the authority to perform numerous patient-related tasks formerly reserved to specialized techs. This gain in autonomy has: (1) Energized the nurses, (2) Improved patient care, (3) Allowed management to cut seven layers of supervision down to four.

Here's a cutting-edge example (also from Bob's book):

> The Mirage and Treasure Island Hotels operate under a system of "planned insubordination." All supervisors must explain to employees not only what to do but why they should do it. If the explanation is not satisfactory, the employee can refuse to do the task.

Sound risky? Well, the risk has had its reward. The hotels have a turnover rate of 12 percent—less than half the industry average.

4. Reciprocate for the greater demands you place on employees.

Notice the various types of job demands. All of these curtail employees' personal lives. Balance this by providing opportunities to deal with personal demands and desires.

- Encourage employees to interact with family and friends during work hours. (We realize that this is in direct opposition to typical practices. But those practices are based on an out-of-date, 9-to-5 paradigm.) Permit personal phone calls. Allow family and friends to access the workplace, and not just an annual Bring Your Son/Daughter to Work Day. And allow employees to access personal e-mail and non-work websites, at least during rest breaks and lunch hours. (Banning access to obscene, violent, or harassing sites is fine, but don't get carried away.)

- Be generous in providing time off to handle personal needs (e.g., doctors' appointments, day-care arrangements, etc.).
- Establish, and encourage use of, an Employee Assistance Program (EAP). We've found that most larger employers have an EAP, usually outsourced, but they insufficiently utilize it. The better EAPs can assist employees with a wide range of personal demands, far beyond alcoholism or drug abuse.
- Encourage employees to establish clubs and special interest groups at work, which meet on the employer's property after hours or during meal breaks. Limit your restrictions on such clubs to just basic human rights violations. For example, ban child pornography and hate groups, but permit men's, women's, and GBL (gay/bisexual/lesbian) groups.

WHAT INDIVIDUALS CAN DO FOR THEMSELVES

There are four arenas of attack available to individuals: physical, mental, interpersonal, and spiritual—our four Cool Tools.

Cool Tool 1: The Physical Arena

This one is pretty straightforward:

1. Get a physical exam—how are burnout and stress impacting your health?
2. Eat healthy—all four food groups, in moderation . . . no fad diets or bingeing.
3. Exercise—regularly, moderately, appropriate to your age and condition.
4. Practice relaxation.

In our workshops, we teach four different relaxation techniques. Here's one of them, called the Purifying Breath:

1. Begin by closing your eyes and just becoming aware of your breathing—without any attempt to modify it. Focus only on your breathing. Tune out any distractions or concerns. Notice your how your belly rises as you breathe in . . . and subsides as you breathe out. Just relax and be with your breathing. Do this for as long as you like.
2. When you're ready, take a deep breath—inhaling slowly through your nose deeply into your abdomen—completely filling your lungs.
3. Hold this breath for as long as you comfortably can.
4. When you're ready, exhale even more slowly through your mouth—pushing all the air out.
5. Repeat steps 2–4 several times.
6. Open your eyes. How do you feel?

Cool Tool 2: The Mental Arena

Ultimately, stress is internally generated—it's how you process external triggers of burnout. Here's how to help:

1. Develop or improve coping skills. These coping skills are perhaps best summarized by the Serenity Prayer, which can be viewed as a religious prayer or a secular self-dedication: "Grant me the serenity to accept the things I cannot change, the courage to change the things I can, and the wisdom to know the difference."
2. Understand your strengths and weaknesses. Capitalize on your strengths and find ways to shore up your weaknesses, e.g., through others and/or self-improvement.
3. Learn effective (not so much time management, but) inner resource management. Take breaks. Relax during your time off (and work breaks). Delegate and/or swap tasks with others. Ask for time off and use all allotted vacation time.
4. Set realistic goals—goals that are important to *you*, not to please others, and are challenging but attainable.
5. Learn to schedule "me" time—not for work, family, or friends, but for you.
6. Consult your EAP (Employee Assistance Program), a life skills coach, or a mental health counselor. You consult professionals for your financial or legal affairs—why not for your mental well-being?

Cool Tool 3: The Interpersonal Arena

Are your relationships with others enhancing the quality of your life or diminishing it?

1. Nurture close relationships—spend quality time with your loved ones.
2. Participate in clubs, associations, and group activities that relax and enrich you. Eliminate the ones that don't.
3. Address ongoing issues with your supervisor, coworkers, family, and friends. Listen to their needs and assert yourself. (Assertion = "This is what I think/ feel/want . . . . How about you?")
4. Consider a job/career/life change. However, avoid making changes out of anger, desperation, or panic. Instead, seek other options—and wait until you can make a logical, rational decision.

Cool Tool 4: The Spiritual Arena

By spiritual, we don't mean anything weird or mystical, rather a cleansing of the soul or nurturing your inner self. It includes:

1. Religion—whatever that may be for you, especially prayer and confession, or their secular counterparts. This may include meditation and support groups.

2. The arts—performing or experiencing music, dance, theater, graphic arts, and so on.
3. Hobbies—that engage your attention and leave you feeling relaxed and fulfilled.
4. Volunteer work—contributing your time to a cause you find meaningful.

STRESS APPLICATION

Think about *your lifestyle* in light of each arena and the specific suggestions included in it. Are there arenas of your life that you've been shortchanging? For example:

- Are you a couch potato? Focus especially on the physical arena.
- Are you a very other-focused person? Concentrate on mental and spiritual arenas.
- Do you keep pretty much to yourself? Focus especially on the interpersonal arena.

Are there *specific aspects* of any arena that ring true for you? For example:

- Are you a very social person? Maybe you need to nurture close relationships more.
- Are you a workaholic? Maybe you need to manage your inner resources more.
- Do you work hard and play hard? Maybe you need to slow down a bit and relax.

Start making changes in your life—gradually, one step at a time. Move especially toward those activities that appeal to you, even if you have to get past some initial resistance. For example:

- If you used to play in a band, don't force yourself to take up stamp collecting. Instead, get back into music.
- If as a child, you loved swimming, get back in the water.
- If you have a solid relationship with your spouse, but no longer feel in love, take a romantic second honeymoon.
- If you used to love reading adventure novels, budget time to do so again.

3. Establish Violence and Weapons Policies

Clearly state the organization's stand on violent, disruptive, and threatening behavior, as well as weapons in the workplace; specify consequences of policy violation. For example:

- Any person who makes threats, exhibits threatening behavior, or engages in violent acts may be removed from the premises pending the outcome of an investigation.
- Threats, threatening behavior, or other acts of violence executed off property but directed at employees or members of the public while conducting official business are a violation of this policy. Off-site threats include but are not limited to threats made via the telephone, fax, electronic or conventional mail, or any other communication medium.
- Violations of this policy will lead to disciplinary action that may include dismissal, arrest, and prosecution. In addition, if the source of such inappropriate behavior is a member of the public, the response may also include barring the person(s) from the premises, termination of business relationships with that individual, and/or prosecution of the person(s).
- Include an incident and warning sign reporting process. [See Key 6.]
- Post the policy at entrances, employment office, and break areas, include it in the employee handbook, and verbally communicate it during new employee orientation, in department meetings, and in training sessions.
- Make sure it is consistently enforced.

See the Sample Policies at the end of this chapter.

4. Use Proper Employee-Selection Techniques

A hiring process that screens out the potentially violent or unstable is an organization's first line of defense. This should include:

- Control by an objective and consistent third party such as HR.
- Review of applications and resumes for behavioral problems, not just skills—for example, gaps in employment/education history, job-hopping, and so on, or anything suspicious or inconsistent.
- Broad background checks (not just criminal record checks) for all jobs.
- Contacting prior employers (i.e., actual supervisors) for all jobs—probing character/behavior-related issues, not just dates of employment or skills.
- Drug and validated psychological testing.
- An in-depth interview of all candidates by HR (looking for behavioral problems) prior to job offer, including behavioral interview questions (e.g., "Give an example of how you performed under stress"—see the sample interview questions at the end of this chapter) and careful probing of the reason for leaving, actual supervisor, title, responsibilities, dates, and issues identified in the application/resume review.
- Effective screening of contract, temporary, and part-time workers.

5. Standardize Discipline and Termination Procedures

- These procedures should preserve the involved employees' dignity, include the tactful and safe handling of high-risk employees and situations (see the Self-Protection Tips in Step 3), and be handled by an objective and consistent third party such as HR.
- Human resources personnel and managers should be trained to identify potential problems among workers, administer discipline as necessary, and terminate employees without causing the terminated employee to feel that the loss of this job is the "end of the line."
- Employee assistance counseling and outplacement services can help employees facing termination for whatever reason. Encourage employees, supervisors, and managers to use these services.
- Conduct exit interviews when employees retire, quit, or are transferred or terminated. Identify potential violence-related problems.

6. Recognize Signs of Trouble, and Ensure They Are Reported

Constantly stay on the alert for the warning signs and triggering events. Establish and communicate reporting and tracking processes:

- For physical violence, verbal abuse, emotional outbursts, threats, strange behavior, and disrespect—not just physical accidents, injuries, and illnesses.
- Offering alternative channels (other than chain of command) for reporting. For example, ombudsman-type managers—representing as much diversity as possible and perceived by most employees as approachable—or an internal or external hotline, with confidentiality safeguards.

7. Investigate All Threats, Complaints, and Red Flags

- Take all specific threats seriously, and find out more about vague threats.
- Pull together your risk assessment team.
- Investigate and interview.
- Talk with the complainant or victim (actual or potential) as soon as possible after the danger has been identified or after an incident has occurred.
- Document what both you and the complainant/victim say. (It may be needed for litigation.)
- Document the threat itself and get statements from others who have heard or observed the perpetrator.
- Meet with the threatener or perpetrator; take his statement; confront with other statements taken; document.

WHAT CONSTITUTES A THREAT?

The definition of a threat for workplace conduct standards need not be the same as the definition of a threat as a criminal offense. A sample definition could be: "An inappropriate behavior, verbal or nonverbal communication, or expression that would lead to the reasonable belief that an act has occurred or may occur that may lead to physical and/or psychological harm to the threatener, to others, or to property." An alternative definition might be: "Any verbal or physical conduct that threatens property or personal safety or that reasonably could be interpreted as intent to cause harm."

A workplace violence prevention program addressing threats needs to include both a subjective and objective component. It must set reasonably explicit standards of behavior so employees know how they are expected to act or not act; it must also make clear to employees that no one has a right to make anyone else feel threatened.

ADDRESSING THREATENING BEHAVIOR

Many times, a violent act is preceded by a threat. The threat may have been explicit or veiled, spoken or unspoken, specific or vague, but it occurred. In other instances, behavior may be observed by others, which might suggest the potential for some type of violent act to occur. In still other cases, it may be an offhanded remark or comments made to people close to the individual that may suggest problematic behavior.

Dealing with threats and/or threatening behavior—detecting them, evaluating them, and finding a way to address them—may be the single most important key to preventing violence.

Any workplace violence strategy must include measures to detect, assess, and manage threats and behavior. Saying that is easier than doing it. It is much easier to deal with a physical assault or homicide than with a threat. Normally there is no doubt that a homicide or assault has been committed; often it is harder to establish that a threat has been made. In addition, the effects of a threat are subjective and subtle; usually there is no physical evidence. Some threats are not criminal and, therefore, not subject to law enforcement intervention and prosecution.

Despite these difficulties, threat response is an essential component of any workplace violence plan.

QUESTIONS TO ASK

As a behavioral consultant to law enforcement, the FBI's National Center for the Analysis of Violent Crime (NCAVC), located at the FBI Academy in Quantico, Virginia, periodically receives requests to assess the risk for violence posed by an individual in a workplace. In some cases, this has been precipitated by a verbal or written threat made in the workplace; at other times it is predicated by unusual or strange behavior and/or comments made to coworkers.

If a communicated threat (verbal, typewritten, e-mailed, or otherwise) is present, an analysis of the verbiage is conducted to determine credibility and viability of the threat. Further, if the offender is unknown, a linguistic profile is developed for investigators, which may identify the offender in the future. In known-offender cases, the analysis of the communicated threats and of the behavior exhibited by the offender is assessed in order to determine the level of threat.

In order to assess this risk, the following suggested questions should be asked to individuals familiar with the offender's behavior, both prior to and after any alleged threat or action.

- Why has the offender threatened, made comments which have been perceived by others as threatening, or taken this action at this particular time? What is happening in the offender's own life that has prompted this?
- What has been said to others, i.e., friends, colleagues, coworkers, etc., regarding what is troubling the offender?
- How does the offender view himself or herself in relation to everyone else?
- Does the offender feel he or she has been wronged in some way?
- Does the offender accept responsibility for his or her own actions?
- How does the offender cope with disappointment, loss, or failure?
- Does the offender blame others for his or her failures?
- How does the offender interact with coworkers?
- Does the offender feel he or she is being treated fairly by the company?
- Does the offender have problems with supervisors or management?
- Is the offender concerned with job practices and responsibilities?
- Has the offender received unfavorable performance reviews or been reprimanded by management?
- Is the offender experiencing personal problems such as divorce, death in the family, health problems, or other personal losses or issues?
- Is the offender experiencing financial problems, high personal debt, or bankruptcy?
- Is there evidence of substance abuse or mental illness/depression?
- Has the offender shown an interest in violence through movies, games, books, or magazines?
- Is the offender preoccupied with violent themes; interested in publicized violent events; or fascinated with and/or has recently acquired weapons?
- Has the offender identified a specific target and communicated with others his or her thoughts or plans for violence?

What Does Not Work?

- one-size-fits-all approach
- rigidity, inflexibility
- denial of problem
- lack of communication with key parties
- lack of collaboration
- ignoring respect
- lack of clear written policy
- lack of careful evaluation of job applicants
- no documentation
- lack of awareness of cultural/diversity issues
- passing around "bad apples"
- lack of an organization-wide commitment to safety

- Is the offender obsessed with others or engaged in any stalking or surveillance activity?
- Has the offender spoken of homicide or suicide?
- Does the offender have a past criminal history or history of past violent behavior?
- Does the offender have a plan for what he or she would do?
- Does the plan make sense? Is it reasonable? Is it specific?
- Does the offender have the means, knowledge, and wherewithal to carry out this plan?

When many of these questions are answered, an accurate picture of the risk for violence is developed, and from this an intervention plan can be devised.

8. Take Appropriate Action

- Communicate with the complainant/victim the results of the investigation and provide support.
- Offer the victim the opportunity for professional counseling and/or security protection.
- Ask the victim what he or she needs from you to increase his or her level of comfort and safety.
- Meet with the threatener or perpetrator again and apply the following as appropriate:
  - Training, coaching, counseling, EAP referral, disciplinary action, termination, arrest
- If appropriate, notify authorities in the community.

9. Train Managers, Employees, and Security Personnel

Training employees in nonviolent response and conflict resolution can reduce the risk that volatile situations will escalate to physical violence. Also critical is training that addresses hazards associated with specific tasks or worksites and relevant prevention strategies. Training should not be regarded as the sole prevention strategy but as a component in a comprehensive approach to reducing workplace violence. To increase vigilance and compliance with stated violence-prevention policies, training should emphasize the appropriate use and maintenance of protective equipment, adherence to administrative controls, and increased knowledge and awareness of the risk of workplace violence.

This training should address:

EMPLOYEES

- workplace violence awareness
- the warning signs of a dangerous employee or customer and the triggering events
- their duty to report all incidents and warning signs, not just overt violence and threats
- how to de-escalate threatening situations
- how to protect themselves and coworkers when threatened
- their responsibility to treat all people with respect and dignity

MANAGERS

- all of the above, plus . . .
- proper discipline and terminations
- their role in incident response and risk assessment
- how to detect the behavioral profile during interviews and reference checks

SECURITY PERSONNEL

- all elements of employee training, plus . . .
- their critical role in incident response
- how to detect potentially dangerous strangers
- appropriate use of physical security measures

10. Conduct a Risk Assessment

A risk assessment should be a constantly evolving process to determine what risks are faced and how they can best be mitigated. How to conduct a risk assessment is described in detail in Step 4.

Case Studies

Having worked your way through this chapter, use the principles you have learned to decide the best course of action in the following cases, taken from the U.S. Office of Personnel Management. They are designed to help you think through similar incidents, and to determine if your prevention and response plans are adequate. (For these and other case studies, see the U.S. Office of Personnel Management's *Dealing with Workplace Violence*, available at www.opm.gov/ employment_and_benefits/worklife/officialdocuments/handbooksguides/ workplaceviolence/full.pdf.)

CASE STUDY 1: STALKING

A supervisor called the employee relations office to request a meeting of the workplace violence team for assistance in handling a situation he's just learned about. He was counseling one of his employees about her frequent unscheduled absences, when she told him a chilling story of what she'd been going through for the past year. She broke up with her boyfriend a year ago and he's been stalking her ever since. He calls her several times a week (she hangs up immediately). He shows up wherever she goes on the weekends and just stares at her from a distance. He often parks his car down the block from her home and just sits there. He's made it known he has a gun.

The organization's plan calls for the initial involvement of security, the Employee Assistance Program (EAP), and employee relations in cases involving stalking. The security officer, the EAP counselor, and employee relations specialist met first with the supervisor and then with the employee and supervisor together. At the meeting with the employee, after learning as much of the background as possible, they gave her some initial suggestions.

- Contact her local police and file a report. Ask them to assess her security at home and make recommendations for improvements.
- Log all future contacts with the stalker and clearly record the date, time, and nature of the contact.
- Let voice mail screen incoming phone calls.
- Contact her own phone company to report the situation.
- Give permission to let her coworkers know what was going on (she would not agree to do this).
- Vary her routines, e.g., go to different shops, take different routes, run errands at different times, report to work on a variable schedule.

The team then worked out the following plan:

- The employee relations specialist acted as coordinator of the response effort. He made a written report of the situation and kept it updated. He kept the team members, the supervisor, and the employee apprised of what the others were doing to resolve the situation. He also looked into the feasibility of relocating the employee to another worksite.

- The security officer immediately reported the situation to the local police. With the employee's consent, she also called the police where the employee lived to learn what steps they could take to help the employee. She offered to coordinate and exchange information with them. The security officer arranged for increased surveillance of the building and circulated photos of the stalker to all building guards with instructions to detain him if he showed up at the building. She brought a tape recorder to the employee's desk and showed her the best way to tape any future voice mail messages from the stalker. She also contacted the phone company to arrange for its involvement in the case.
- The counselor provided support and counseling for both the employee and the supervisor throughout the time this was going on. He suggested local organizations that could help the employee. He also tried to convince her to tell coworkers about the situation.
- The union arranged to sponsor a session on stalking in order to raise the consciousness of employees about the problem in general.

After a week, when the employee finally agreed to tell coworkers what was going on, the counselor and security officer jointly held a meeting with the whole work group to discuss any fears or concerns they had and give advice on how they could help with the situation.

In this case, the employee's coworkers were supportive and wanted to help out. They volunteered to watch out for the stalker and to follow other security measures recommended by the security specialist. The stalker ended up in jail because he tried to break into the employee's home while armed with a gun. The security officer believes that the local police were able to be more responsive in this situation because they had been working together with office security on the case.

Questions for the planning group

- Do you agree with the organization's approach in this case?
- What would you do in a similar situation if your organization doesn't have security guards?
- What would you do if coworkers were too afraid of the stalker to work in the same office with the employee?
- What would you do if/when the stalker gets out of jail on bail or out on probation?
- Would your organization's attorney or security officer have gotten involved in this case—for example, coordinated its efforts with local law enforcement agencies?

CASE STUDY 2: THREAT OF VIOLENCE

At a smoking break with one of his colleagues from down the hall, an employee was reported to have said, "I like the way some employees handle problems with their supervisors—they eliminate them. One of these days I'm going to bring in my gun and take care of my problem." The employee who heard the statement reported it to his supervisor, who in turn reported it to his supervisor, who called a member of the workplace violence team.

In the case of a reported threat where there does not appear to be an imminent danger, the organization's plan called for the employee relations specialist to conduct an immediate preliminary investigation and for the team to meet with the supervisor immediately afterward to look at the available evidence and strategize a preliminary response.

That afternoon, the employee relations specialist interviewed the employee who heard the threat, that employee's supervisor, the supervisor of the employee who made the threat, and subsequently the employee who allegedly made the threat. The employee who made the threat denied saying any such thing. There were no witnesses.

The supervisor of the employee who allegedly made the threat reported that, several months earlier, the same employee had responded to his casual question about weekend plans by saying, "I'm going to spend the weekend in my basement with my guns practicing my revenge." At that time, the supervisor had warned the employee that such talk was unacceptable at work and referred the employee to the organization's written policy. . . .

The security officer and the employee's second-level supervisor went together to give the alleged threatener a letter that stated, "This is to inform you that effective immediately you will be in a paid, nonduty status, pending a determination regarding your actions on June 10. You are required to provide a phone number where you can be reached during working hours." . . .

The investigative report showed that the employee told his coworkers on several occasions that he had no respect for his supervisor and that he thought that threatening him was an effective way to solve his problems with him. Signed statements indicated that he bragged about knowing how to get his way with his boss. . . . The team recommended he be terminated, as he was using threats to intimidate his supervisor. . . .

The employee was soon hired by another organization, which never checked his references and is now experiencing the same type of intimidating behavior from the employee.

Questions for the planning group

• What would your organization have done about checking references before hiring this employee?

- Would your organization have removed the employee or taken some other course of action?
- How would your organization have handled the case if the key witness (i.e., the employee who heard the threat) had demonstrated certain behavior that cast doubt on his credibility?

CASE STUDY 3: THREATENING BEHAVIOR

A visibly upset male employee cornered a female employee in her office, and said quietly and slowly that she will pay with her life for going over his head to ask about his work. The male employee then stared at his coworker with his hands clenched rigidly at this side before leaving the office and slamming the door behind him. The female employee, fearful and shaken, reported this to her supervisor, who immediately reported the incident to the director of employee relations.

The organization's response plan calls for involvement of employee relations, security, and the Employee Assistance Program (EAP) in cases involving threats. Immediately following the report to the response team, the security officer contacted the female employee to assist her in filing a police report on the threat and to discuss safety measures that she should be taking. The victim was also referred to counseling, where she also received educational materials on handling severe stress.

An investigation was immediately conducted. In her statement, the female employee repeated what she had reported to the supervisor earlier about the threat. In his statement, the male employee stated that, on the day in question, he had been upset about what he felt were some underhanded activities by the female employee and his only recollection about the conversation was that he made a general statement like "You'll pay" to her. He stated that this was not a threat, just an expression. The investigation showed that the employee had several previous incidents of intimidating behavior that had resulted in disciplinary action.

After reviewing the results of the investigation, the supervisor proposed a removal action, finding that the female employee's version of the incident was more credible. In his response to the proposed notice, the employee brought in medical documentation that said he had a psychiatric disability of post-traumatic stress disorder, which caused his misconduct, and he requested a reasonable accommodation. The deciding official consulted with a company attorney and employee relations specialist, who explained that nothing in the Rehabilitation Act prohibits an organization from maintaining a workplace free of threats of violence. Further, they explained that a request for reasonable accommodation does not excuse employee misconduct nor does it shield an employee from discipline. The deciding official determined that removal was the appropriate discipline in this case. The employee did not appeal the action.

Questions for the planning group

- Do you agree with the organization's approach in this case?
- If this situation occurred at your organization, would you have involved law enforcement early in the process?
- Who would conduct the investigation at your organization?
- What else would your organization have done to protect the employee?
- Would you have requested more medical documentation from the employee?
- What risks must be balanced when selecting a penalty?

CASE STUDY 4: THREAT TO KILL

The first incident report that came in to the newly formed workplace violence team was from a field office. Two months after an employee retired on disability retirement, he began threatening his ex-supervisor. He knocked on his ex-supervisor's apartment door late one evening. He left threatening statements on the supervisor's home answering machine, such as "I just wanted to let you know I bought a gun." On one occasion, a psychiatrist called the supervisor and the security office and told them that the ex-employee had threatened to murder his ex-supervisor. The psychiatrist said the threat should be taken seriously, especially because he was drinking heavily. A coworker received an anonymous letter stating, "It is not over with [name of supervisor]."

Each time a threat was reported, the security office took extra measures to protect the supervisor while at the workplace and the supervisor reported the incident to the local police. Each time, the supervisor was informed that the police were unable to take action on the threats because they did not rise to a criminal level. The supervisor spoke with the county magistrate about a restraining order, but again was told the threats did not rise to the level required to obtain a restraining order.

The workplace violence team held a conference call with the threatened supervisor, the director of the office, and the security chief of the field office. They suggested the following actions.

Recommendations for the security officer

- Confirm the whereabouts of the ex-employee and periodically reconfirm his whereabouts.
- Meet with local police to determine whether the ex-employee's behavior constitutes a crime in the jurisdiction and whether other applicable charges

(such as stalking or harassment) might be considered. Ask if the police department has a threat assessment unit or access to one at the state level. Ask police about contacting the U.S. Postal Service for assistance in tracing the anonymous letter (18 USC 876).

- Meet with the psychiatrist who called the organization and ask him to send a letter to the chief of police reporting the threats. Also, inform the psychiatrist about the ex-employee's behavior and discuss whether or not involuntary hospitalization might be an option. Attempt to establish an ongoing dialogue with the psychiatrist and try to get a commitment from him to share information about the case to the extent allowed by confidentiality.
- Provide periodic updates to the threatened supervisor on the status of the case, actions taken, and actions being contemplated.
- Provide support and advice to the threatened supervisor, including telephone numbers and points of contact for local telephone company, local law enforcement, and local victim assistance organizations.

Recommendations for the director of the field office

- Meet with security and police to consider options (and their ramifications) for encouraging the ex-employee to cease and desist his threatening activities.
- Provide support to the supervisor by encouraging the supervisor to utilize the Employee Assistance Program.

Recommendations for the threatened supervisor

- Keep detailed notes about each contact with the ex-employee. Give copies of all the notes to the police. (They explained to the supervisor that in all probability, each time he went to the police, it was treated like a new report, and thus, as individual incidents, they did not rise to the level of a crime.)
- Contact the phone company to alert them to the situation.
- Tape record all messages left on the answering machine
- Contact the local office of victim assistance for additional ideas.

Contact with the local police confirmed that each report had been taken as a new case. When presented with the cumulative evidence, in fact, the ex-employee's behavior did rise to the level of stalking under state law. The police visited the ex-employee and warned him that further threats could result in an arrest. At the threatened supervisor's request, the county magistrate issued a restraining order prohibiting personal contact and any continued communication. Two months after the restraining order was issued, the ex-employee was arrested for breaking the restraining order.

The security office and the supervisor kept in contact with the police about the case to reduce any further risk of violence.

Questions for the planning group

- Do you think the organization's approach in this case was adequate to protect the supervisor?
- Have you already established liaison with appropriate law enforcement authorities to ensure that situations such as this get the proper attention from the beginning?
- What would your organization do if the psychiatrist refused to get involved?
- Are there any laws in your state requiring mental health professionals to protect potential victims when threats have been made?
- How would you continue to monitor the ex-employee's activities after he is released from jail?
- What would your organization do if the case continued without the ex-employee being arrested?

CASE STUDY 5: INTIMIDATION

A supervisor reported to an HR specialist that he recently heard from one of his employees (alleged victim) that another one of his employees (alleged perpetrator) had been intimidating him with his "in your face" behavior. The alleged perpetrator had stood over the alleged victim's desk in what the alleged victim perceived as a menacing way, physically crowded him out in an elevator, and made menacing gestures. The supervisor stated that the alleged perpetrator was an average performer, somewhat of a loner, but there were no behavior problems that he was aware of until the employee came to him expressing his fear. He said that the employee who reported the situation said he did not want the supervisor to say anything to anyone, so the supervisor tried to observe the situation for a couple of days. When he didn't observe any of the behavior described, he spoke with the alleged victim again and told him he would consult with the crisis management team.

In cases involving reports of intimidation, this organization's crisis response plan called for involvement of Human Resources (HR) and the Employee Assistance Program (EAP) (with the clear understanding that they would contact other resources as needed).

The first thing the HR specialist did was to set up a meeting for the next day with the supervisor, an EAP counselor, and another HR specialist who was skilled in conflict resolution.

At that meeting, several options were discussed. One was to initiate an immediate investigation into the allegations, which would involve interviewing the alleged victim, any witnesses identified by the alleged victim, and the alleged perpetrator.

Another suggestion offered by the EAP counselor was that, in view of the alleged victim's reluctance to speak up about it, they could arrange a training session for the entire office on conflict resolution (at which time the EAP counselor could observe the dynamics of the entire work group). The EAP counselor noted that conflict resolution classes were regularly scheduled at the organization. The supervisor also admitted that he was aware of a lot of tensions in the office and would like the EAP's assistance in resolving whatever was causing them.

After discussing the options, the supervisor and the team decided to try the conflict resolution training session before initiating an investigation.

At the training session, during some of the exercises, it became clear that the alleged victim contributed significantly to the tension between the two employees. The alleged victim, in fact, seemed to contribute significantly to conflicts not only with the alleged perpetrator, but with his coworkers as well. The alleged perpetrator seemed to react assertively, but not inappropriately, to the alleged victim's attempts to annoy him.

Office tensions were reduced to minimum as a result of the training session and follow-up work by the Employee Assistance Program. The employee who initially reported the intimidation to his supervisor not only realized what he was doing to contribute to office tensions, but he also actively sought help to change his approach and began to conduct himself more effectively with his coworkers. He appreciated getting the situation resolved in a low-key way that did not cause him embarrassment and began to work cooperatively with the alleged perpetrator. The alleged perpetrator never learned about the original complaint, but he did learn from the training session more effective ways to conduct himself with his coworkers. This incident took place over a year ago, and the organization reports that both are productive team players.

Questions for the planning group

- Do you agree with the organization's approach in this situation?
- Can you think of other situations that could be addressed effectively through an intervention with the work group?
- In what kinds of situations would this approach be counterproductive?
- Can you envision a scenario where using the group conflict resolution session to get at any individualized problem might have a negative, rather than a positive, effect?
- Has your organization conducted employee training on such topics as conflict resolution, stress management, and dealing with hostile persons?

CASE STUDY 6: FRIGHTENING BEHAVIOR

A supervisor contacted the employee relations office because one of his employees was making the other employees in the office uncomfortable. He said the employee did not seem to have engaged in any actionable misconduct but, because of the organization's new workplace violence policy, and the workplace violence training he had just received, he thought he should at least mention what was going on.

The employee was recently divorced and had been going through a difficult time for over two years; he had made it clear that he was having financial problems that were causing him to be stressed out. He was irritable and aggressive in his speech much of the time. He would routinely talk about the number of guns he owned, not in the same sentence, but in the same general conversation in which he would mention that someone else was causing all of his problems.

At the first meeting with the supervisor, the employee relations specialist and Employee Assistance Program (EAP) counselor suggested that, since this was a long-running situation rather than an immediate crisis, the supervisor would have time to do some fact-finding. They gave him several suggestions on how to do this while safeguarding the privacy of the employee (for example, request a confidential conversation with previous supervisors, go back to coworkers who registered complaints for more information, and, if he was not already familiar with his personnel records, pull his file to see if there were any previous adverse actions in it). Two days later they had another meeting to discuss the case and strategize a plan of action.

The supervisor's initial fact-finding showed that the employee's coworkers attributed his aggressive behavior to the difficult divorce situation he had been going through, but they were nevertheless afraid of him. The supervisor did not learn any more specifics about why they were afraid, except that he was short-tempered, ill-mannered, and spoke a lot about his guns (although, according to the coworkers, in a matter-of-fact rather than in an intimidating manner).

After getting ideas from the employee relations specialist and the counselor, the supervisor sat down with the employee and discussed his behavior. He told the employee it was making everyone uncomfortable and that it must stop. He referred the employee to the EAP, setting a time and date to meet with the counselor.

As a result of counseling by the supervisor and by the EAP counselor, the employee changed his behavior. He was unaware that his behavior was scaring people. He learned new ways from the EAP to deal with people. He accepted the EAP referral to a therapist in the community to address underlying personal problems. Continued monitoring by the supervisor showed the employee's conduct improving to an acceptable level and remaining that way.

Questions for the planning group

- Do you agree with the organization's approach in this case?
- Can you think of other situations that would lend themselves to this kind of low-key approach?

• Does your organization have effective EAP training so that supervisors are comfortable in turning to the EAP for advice?

CASE STUDY 7: DISRUPTIVE BEHAVIOR

After workplace violence training was conducted at the company, during which early intervention was emphasized, an employee called a member of the workplace violence team for advice on dealing with his senior coworker. He said the coworker, who had been hired six months earlier, was in the habit of shouting and making demeaning remarks to the other employees in the office.

The senior coworker was skilled in twisting words around and manipulating situations to his advantage. For example, when employees would ask him for advice on a topic in his area of expertise, he would tell them to use their own common sense. Then when they finished the assignment, he would make demeaning remarks about them and speak loudly about how they had done their work the wrong way. At other times, he would demand rudely in a loud voice that they drop whatever they were working on and help him with his project. The employee said he had attempted to speak with his supervisor about the situation, but was told not to make a mountain out of a mole hill.

The EAP counselor met with the employee who had reported the situation. The employee described feelings of being overwhelmed and helpless. The demeaning remarks were becoming intolerable.

The employee believed that attempts to resolve the issue with the coworker were futile. The fact that the supervisor minimized the situation further discouraged the employee. By the end of the meeting with the counselor, however, the employee was able to recognize that not saying anything was not helping and was actually allowing a bad situation to get worse.

At a subsequent meeting, the EAP counselor and the employee explored skills to address the situation in a respectful, reasonable, and responsible manner with both his supervisor and the abusive coworker. The counselor suggested using language such as:

"I don't like shouting. Please lower your voice."
"I don't like it when you put me down in front of my peers."
"It's demeaning when I am told that I am . . ."
"I don't like it when you point your finger at me."
"I want to have a good working relationship with you."

The employee learned to focus on his personal professionalism and responsibility to establish and maintain reasonable boundaries and limits by using these types of firm and friendly "I statements," acknowledging that he heard and understood what the supervisor and coworker were saying, and repeating what he needed to communicate to them.

After practicing with the EAP counselor, the employee was able to discuss the situation again with his supervisor. He described the situation in nonblaming terms, and he expressed his intentions to work at improving the situation. The supervisor acknowledged that the shouting was annoying, but again asked the employee not to make a mountain out of a mole hill. The employee took a deep breath and said, "It may be a mole hill, but nevertheless it is affecting my ability to get my work done efficiently." Finally, the supervisor stated that he did not realize how disruptive the situation had become and agreed to monitor the situation.

The next time the coworker raised his voice, the employee used his newly acquired assertiveness skills and stated in a calm and quiet voice, "I don't like to be shouted at. Please lower your voice." When the coworker started shouting again, the employee restated in a calm voice, "I don't like being shouted at. Please lower your voice." The coworker stormed away.

Meanwhile, the supervisor began monitoring the situation. He noted that the abusive coworker's conduct had improved with the newly assertive employee, but continued to be rude and demeaning toward the other employees. The supervisor consulted with the EAP counselor and employee relations specialist. The counselor told him, "Generally, people don't change unless they have a reason to change." The counselor added that the reasons people change can range from simple "I statements," such as those suggested above, to disciplinary actions. The employee relations specialist discussed possible disciplinary options with the supervisor.

The supervisor then met with the abusive coworker, who blamed the altercations on the others in the office. The supervisor responded, "I understand the others were stressed. I'm glad you understand that shouting, speaking in a demeaning manner, and rudely ordering people around is unprofessional and disrespectful. It is unacceptable behavior and will not be tolerated." During the meeting, he also referred the employee to the Employee Assistance Program.

The coworker continued his rude and demeaning behavior to the other employees in spite of the supervisor's efforts. The others, after observing the newly acquired confidence and calm of the employee who first raised the issue, requested similar training from the EAP. The supervisor met again with the EAP counselor and employee relations specialist to strategize next steps.

When all of the employees in the office started using assertive statements, the abusive coworker became more cooperative. However, it took a written reprimand, a short suspension, and several counseling sessions with the EAP counselor before he ceased his shouting and rude behavior altogether.

Questions for the planning group

- Does your workplace violence training include communication skills to put a stop to disruptive behavior early on (including skills for convincing reluctant supervisors to act)?
- How would your organization have proceeded with the case if the coworker had threatened the employee who spoke to him in an assertive way?
- What recourse would the employee have had if the supervisor had refused to intervene?

CASE STUDY 8: THREAT ASSESSMENT

The following is an account (from the FBI's *Workplace Violence* manual) of a threat assessment conducted jointly by a criminal investigator and a mental health professional.

During a training session, the forty-six-year-old subject made comments regarding his alcoholism, causing such a disturbance that he was subsequently referred to the employee assistance counseling program. On two other occasions, he displayed inappropriate behavior by storming around the office, cursing, and throwing objects. In another training workshop, he made verbally abusive comments, disturbing the class.

After a month's leave, he had a verbal outburst during a meeting on his first day back in the office and requested a transfer due to stress. The request was denied. He then requested more leave, which was granted. The subject was noticeably withdrawn and his performance declined. Supervisors documented a pattern of unusual agitation over minor issues, unreasonable complaints, unacceptable work, and allegations that coworkers were conspiring against him. The subject was voluntarily hospitalized twice for homicidal ideations. He was treated for psychosis and suicidal and paranoid delusions associated with his coworkers. His physician recommended a disability retirement. A month before his disability pension was approved he began to leave harassing voicemail messages on a coworker's telephone. An example of the messages is: "Hi, Darlene, it's Stan. Just wanted to say Happy Thanksgiving. And, you give this message to Yvonne. Tell her if she had been off the property the day she hollered at me, I would have beat her m_____ f_____ ass. Bye, Darlene."

He was diagnosed with delusional disorder, paranoid type. This information was also provided to law enforcement during the investigation.

His retirement papers contained disturbing comments. For example, recalling a meeting with a Human Resources staff member, he said: "I started to grab her by the throat and choke her, until the top part of her head popped off. Then I was going to step on her throat and pluck her bozo hairdo bald. Strand by strand . . . ."

Some months later, the subject told a former coworker that he was following a former supervisor and her family. He provided specific information, stating that he knew where some of the targets lived and the types and colors of vehicles they drove. The subject also made comments about the target's family members and stated that he had three guns for each of his former supervisors.

At this point, law enforcement was notified. While the police investigation was under way, the subject made threats against five former female coworkers. A threat assessment was conducted analyzing letters, voicemails, reports from EAP, and interviews with various individuals. The subject's communications were organized and contained specific threats. For example, he wrote, "Don't let the passage of time fool you, all is not forgotten or forgiven" and "I will in my own time strike again, and it will be unmerciful." The material suggested that he was becoming increasingly fixated on the targets, and his communications articulated an action imperative that suggested that the risk was increasing. After obtaining additional information, the investigators informed the subject of specific limits and consequences that would occur if he continued his threatening behavior and communications. The subject assured law enforcement agents that his intent was to pursue legal reparations.

Four months later, however, he mailed letters to his five targets stating that he wanted to "execute" one of them. The letters indicated that he was close to committing an attack. Based on the ongoing assessment and insight into his thinking and behavior over several months, the threat assessment team, consisting of an investigator and a mental health professional, initiated a conference call with the district attorney. In the conference, the mental health professional provided an assessment of the subject's potential for violence, and the investigator presented evidence regarding the laws violated and law enforcement actions taken to date.

The threat assessment report, along with other evidence, was used by the district attorney in obtaining an arrest and search warrant. The final recommendation by the team was that the subject should be arrested and held without bond. Six months after the arrest, he was found not guilty by reason of insanity.

See figures 5.1, 5.2, and 5.3 for sample written policy statements. For an example of a completed workplace violence prevention program, see the end of this chapter.

Sample Written Policy Statement A

This organization does not tolerate workplace violence. We define workplace violence as actions or words that endanger or harm another employee or result in other employees having a reasonable belief that they are in danger. Such actions include:

- Verbal or physical harassment
- Verbal or physical threats
- Assaults or other violence
- Any other behavior that causes others to feel unsafe (e.g., bullying, sexual harassment)
- Company policy requires an immediate response to all reports of violence. All threatening incidents will be investigated and documented by the employee relations department.

If appropriate, the company may provide counseling services or referrals for employees. The following disciplinary actions may also be taken:

- Oral reprimand
- Written reprimand
- Suspension
- Termination

It's the responsibility of all employees to report all threatening behavior to management immediately. The goal of this policy is to promote the safety and well-being of all people in our workplace.

Sample Written Policy Statement B

MEMORANDUM FOR EMPLOYEES OF _____
FROM: [Department or Agency Head]
SUBJECT: Workplace Violence

It is the [*insert name*]'s policy to promote a safe environment for its employees. We are committed to working with our employees to maintain a work environment free from violence, threats of violence, harassment, intimidation, and other disruptive behavior. While this kind of conduct is not pervasive at our organization, we are not immune. Every organization will be affected by disruptive behavior at one time or another.

Violence, threats, harassment, intimidation, and other disruptive behavior in our workplace will not be tolerated; that is, all reports of incidents will be taken seriously and will be dealt with appropriately. Such behavior can include oral or written statements, gestures, or expressions that communicate a direct or indirect threat of physical harm. Individuals who commit such acts may be removed from the premises and may be subject to disciplinary action or criminal penalties.

We need your cooperation to implement this policy effectively and maintain a safe working environment. Do not ignore violent, threatening, harassing, intimidating, or other disruptive behavior. If you observe or experience such behavior by anyone on agency premises, whether he or she is an employee or not, report it immediately to a supervisor or manager. Supervisors and managers who receive such reports should seek advice from the Employee Relations Office at xxx-xxxx regarding investigating the incident and initiating appropriate action.

PLEASE NOTE: Threats or assaults that require immediate attention by security or police should be reported first to security at xxx-xxxx or to police at 911.

I will support all efforts made by supervisors in dealing with violent, threatening, harassing, intimidating, or other disruptive behavior in our workplace and will monitor whether this policy is being implemented effectively. If you have any questions about this policy statement, please contact _____ at xxx-xxxx.

Sample Written Policy Statement C

[Effective Date for Program]

Our establishment, [Employer Name], is concerned and committed to our employees' safety and health. We refuse to tolerate violence in the workplace and will make every effort to prevent violent incidents from occurring by implementing a Workplace Violence Prevention (WPVP) Program. We will provide adequate authority and budgetary resources to responsible parties so that our goals and responsibilities can be met.

All managers and supervisors are responsible for implementing and maintaining our WPVP Program. We encourage employee participation in designing and implementing our program. We require prompt and accurate reporting of all violent incidents, whether or not physical injury has occurred. We will not discriminate against victims of workplace violence.

A copy of this policy statement and our WPVP program is readily available to all employees from each manager and supervisor.

Our program ensures that all employees, including supervisors and managers, adhere to work practices that are designed to make the workplace more secure, and do not engage in verbal threats or physical actions which create a security hazard for others in the workplace.

All employees, including managers and supervisors, are responsible for using safe work practices; for following all directives, policies, and procedures; and for assisting in maintaining a safe and secure work environment.

The management of our establishment is responsible for ensuring that all safety and health policies and procedures involving workplace security are clearly communicated and understood by all employees. Managers and supervisors are expected to enforce the rules fairly and uniformly.

Our program will be reviewed and updated annually.

Sample Weapons Policy

In order to ensure a safe environment for employees and customers, our establishment, *(employer name)* prohibits the wearing, transporting, storage, or presence of firearms or other dangerous weapons in our facilities or on our property. Any employee in possession of a firearm or other weapon while on our facilities/property or while otherwise fulfilling job responsibilities may face disciplinary action including termination. A client or visitor who violates this policy may be removed from the property and reported to police authorities. Possession of a valid concealed weapons permit is *not* an exemption under this policy.

DEFINITION

"Firearms or other dangerous weapons" means

- any device from which a projectile may be fired by an explosive
- any simulated firearm operated by gas or compressed air
- slingshot
- sand club
- metal knuckles
- any spring-blade knife
- any knife that opens or is ejected open by an outward, downward thrust or movement
- any instrument that can be used as a club and poses a reasonable risk of injury

EXEMPTIONS

This policy does not apply to

- any law enforcement personnel engaged in official duties
- any security personnel engaged in official duties
- any person engaged in military activities sponsored by the federal or state government, while engaged in official duties

NOTIFICATION

"No Firearms or Other Dangerous Weapons" signs shall be conspicuously posted within all (employer name) facilities and in parking areas and grounds surrounding our facilities. These signs will clearly indicate that firearms and other weapons are not to be carried onto our property or into our facilities.

REPORTING

Staff or security personnel will request any visitor found in possession of a firearm or other dangerous weapon to remove it from the facility, and local law enforcement authorities will be notified promptly.

SPECIAL INSTRUCTIONS FOR EMPLOYEES

Any employee concerned about personal safety may request an escort (e.g., to a parking lot off premises) or other appropriate intervention by security personnel. Educational materials will be made available on request regarding the magnitude of the workplace violence problem in the United States and the role of firearms and other dangerous weapons in this violence. Training will be provided to employees on this and other workplace violence prevention measures that (employer name) has implemented.

Sample Domestic Violence in the Workplace Policy

DESCRIPTION

Domestic violence is abusive behavior that is either physical, sexual, and/or psychological, intended to establish and maintain control over a partner. Domestic violence is a serious problem that affects people from all walks of life. It can adversely affect the well-being and productivity of employees who are victims, as well as their coworkers. Other effects of domestic violence in the workplace include increased absenteeism, turnover, health-care costs, and reduced productivity.

POLICY STATEMENT

(Employer name) will not tolerate domestic violence including harassment of any employee or client while in our facilities or vehicles, on our property, or while conducting business. This includes the display of any violent or threatening behavior (verbal or physical) that may result in physical or emotional injury or otherwise places one's safety and productivity at risk.

Any employee who threatens, harasses, or abuses someone at our workplace or from the workplace using any company resources such as work time, workplace phones, fax machines, mail, e-mail, or other means may be subject to corrective or disciplinary action, up to and including dismissal. Corrective or disciplinary action may also be taken against employees who are arrested, convicted, or issued a permanent injunction as a result of domestic violence when such action has a direct connection to the employee's duties in our company.

(Employer name) is committed to working with employees who are victims of domestic violence to prevent abuse and harassment from occurring in the workplace. No employees will be penalized or disciplined solely for being a victim of harassment in the workplace. Our company will provide appropriate support and assistance to employees who are victims of domestic violence. This includes confidential means for coming forward for help; resource and referral information; work schedule adjustments or leave as needed to obtain assistance; and workplace relocation as feasible.

Employees who are perpetrators of domestic violence are also encouraged to seek assistance. Our company will provide information regarding counseling and certified treatment resources, and make work schedule arrangements to receive such assistance.

Components of a Domestic Violence Workplace Safety Plan

- Consider obtaining civil orders for protection and make sure that they remain current and are in hand at all times. A copy should be provided to the employee's supervisor, the reception area, and security areas if there is a concern about the abusive partner coming to the worksite.
- The employee should consider providing a picture of the perpetrator to reception areas and/or security.
- A company contact person should be identified for the employee to reach when needed.
- An emergency contact person should be identified should the employer be unable to contact the employee.
- Review the employee's parking arrangements for possible changes.
- Consider changing the employee's work schedule.
- Consider what steps need to be taken to provide for the safety of other employees and clients.
- Consider having the employee's telephone calls screened at work.

Sample Behavior-Based Pre-employment Interview Questions

1. Tell me about the worst disagreement you have had with a coworker or boss.
   - What did each of you say?
   - What was the discussion like when it was the most heated?
   - How did both of you show your frustration or anger?
   - How was it resolved?
   - How was your relationship with that person after the incident?
2. When have you needed to coordinate with another employee, unit, or other organization?
   - What did you do to facilitate coordination and cooperation?
   - What difficulties did you encounter?
   - How did you handle them?
   - What was the outcome?
3. You have heard the phrase "Shoot from the hip." Tell me about a time you had to do that.
   - Describe the situation.
   - How did it turn out?
   - Were you comfortable in that situation?
4. Tell me about a time when you were in the middle of a project and a manager stopped you abruptly and redirected most or all your efforts to a new assignment.
   - What happened?

5. What types of things have made you angry, and how did you react to them?
6. You know the expression "roll with the punches." Tell me about a time when you had to do that when dealing with a person.
7. Describe a time when you communicated some unpleasant feeling to a supervisor.
   • What happened?
8. What experience have you had with a miscommunication with a customer or coworker?
   • Tell me how you solved the problem.

Employee Security Survey

This survey will help detect security problems in your building or at an alternate worksite. Please fill out this form, get your coworkers to fill it out and review it to see where the potential for major security problems lies.

NAME: _____

WORK LOCATION: _____
(IN BUILDING OR ALTERNATE WORKSITE)

1. Do either of these two conditions exist in your building or at your alternate worksite?

   ❑ Work alone during working hours.
   ❑ No notification given to anyone when you finish work.

   Are these conditions a problem? If so, please describe when. (For example, Mondays, evening, daylight savings time.) _____

2. Do you have any of the following complaints (which may be associated with causing an unsafe worksite)? (Check all that apply.)

   ❑ Does your workplace have a written policy to follow for addressing general problems?
   ❑ Does your workplace have a written policy on
      • How to handle a violent client
      • When and how to request the assistance of a coworker
      • When and how to request the assistance of police
      • What to do about a verbal threat
      • What to do about a threat of violence
      • What to do about harassment
      • Working alone
      • Alarm system(s)
      • Security in and out of building
      • Security in parking lot

❏ Have you been assaulted by a coworker?

❏ To your knowledge, have incidents of violence ever occurred between your coworkers?

3. Are violence-related incidents worse during shift work, on the road, or in other situations? Please specify. _____

4. Where in the building or worksite would a violence-related incident most likely occur?

❏ lounge

❏ exits

❏ deliveries

❏ private offices

❏ parking lot

❏ bathroom

❏ entrance

❏ other (specify)

5. Have you ever noticed a situation that could have led to a violent incident?

6. Have you missed work because of a potential violent act(s) committed during your course of employment?

7. Do you receive workplace violence-related training or assistance of any kind?

8. Has anything happened recently at your worksite that could have led to violence? Can you comment about the situation?

9. Has the number of violent clients increased?

Sample Completed WPVP Program
(courtesy of Long Island Coalition for
Workplace Violence Awareness and Prevention)

ABC COMPANY'S WPVP PROGRAM POLICY STATEMENT
JANUARY 1, 2008

Our establishment, **ABC Company,** is concerned and committed to our employees' safety and health. We refuse to tolerate violence in the workplace and will make every effort to prevent violent incidents from occurring by implementing a workplace violence prevention program (WPVP). We will provide adequate authority and budgetary resources to responsible parties so that our goals and responsibilities can be met.

All managers and supervisors are responsible for implementing and maintaining our WPVP program. We encourage employee participation in designing and implementing our program. We require prompt and accurate reporting of all violent incidents whether or not physical injury has occurred. We will not discriminate against victims of workplace violence.

A copy of this policy statement and our WPVP program is readily available to all employees from each manager and supervisor.

Our program ensures that all employees, including supervisors and managers, adhere to work practices that are designed to make the workplace more secure, and do not engage in verbal threats or physical actions that create a security hazard for others in the workplace.

All employees, including managers and supervisors, are responsible for using safe work practices, for following all directives, policies and procedures, and for assisting in maintaining a safe and secure work environment.

The management of our establishment is responsible for ensuring that all safety and health policies and procedures involving workplace security are clearly communicated and understood by all employees. Managers and supervisors are expected to enforce the rules fairly and uniformly.

Our program will be reviewed and updated annually.

WORKPLACE VIOLENCE PREVENTION PROGRAM RISK ASSESSMENT TEAM

A risk assessment team will be established, and part of their duties will be to assess the vulnerability to workplace violence at our establishment and reach agreement on preventive actions to be taken. They will be responsible for auditing our overall workplace violence prevention program.

The risk assessment team will consist of:

Name:	Title:	Phone:
John Smith	**Vice President**	**555-1212**
Jane Doe	**Operations**	**555-1234**
Frank Kras	**Shop Steward**	**555-1233**
James Brown	**Security**	**555-1456**
Susan Dean	**Treasurer**	**555-1567**
Tom Jones	**Legal Counsel**	**555-1678**
Sally Field	**Personnel**	**555-1789**

The team will develop employee training programs in violence prevention and plan for responding to acts of violence. They will communicate this plan internally to all employees.

The risk assessment team will begin its work by reviewing previous incidents of violence at our workplace. They will analyze and review existing records identifying patterns that may indicate causes and severity of assault incidents and identify changes necessary to correct these hazards. These records include, but are not limited to, OSHA 200 logs, past incident reports, medical records, insurance records, workers' compensation records, police reports, accident investigations, training records, grievances, minutes of meetings, and so on. The team will communicate with similar local businesses and trade associates concerning their experiences with workplace violence.

Additionally, they will inspect the workplace and evaluate the work tasks of all employees to determine the presence of hazards, conditions, operations, and other situations that might place our workers at risk of occupational assault incidents. Employees will be surveyed to identify the potential for violent incidents and to identify or confirm the need for improved security measures. These surveys shall be reviewed, updated, and distributed as needed or at least once within a two-year period.

Periodic inspections to identify and evaluate workplace security hazards and risks of workplace violence will be performed by the following representatives of the assessment team, in the following areas of our workplace:

Representative: **John Smith**   Area: **General Office**
Representative: **Frank Kras**   Area: **Shop and Lab**
Representative: **Jane Doe**   Area: **Reception and Sales**

Periodic inspections will be performed according to the following schedule:

First Monday of Every Month
(frequency: daily, weekly, monthly, etc.)

HAZARD ASSESSMENT

On **September 5, 2008**, the risk assessment team completed the hazard assessment. This consisted of a records review, inspection of the worksite, and employee survey.

Records Review. The risk assessment team reviewed the following records:

- OSHA 200 logs for the last three years
- Incident reports
- Records of or information compiled for recording of assault incidents or near-assault incidents
- Insurance records
- Police reports
- Accident investigations
- Training records
- Grievances
- Other relevant records or information: **workers' compensation records.**

From these records, we have identified the following issues that need to be addressed:

- Employees have been assaulted by irate clients.
- Employees have been assaulted while traveling alone.
- There have been several incidents of assault and harassment among employees.

WORKPLACE SECURITY ANALYSIS

Inspection: The risk assessment team inspected the workplace on **July 31, 2008**. From this inspection the following issues have been identified:

- Access to the building is not controlled, and it is not limited to any of the offices on the four floors that we occupy. There have been problems with nonemployees entering private work areas.
- Doors to the restrooms are not kept locked.
- Lighting in the parking lot is inadequate.
- In client service area, desks are situated in a way that make it necessary for employees to walk past the client in order to leave the area. There are many objects on top of desks that could be used as weapons (e.g., scissors, stapler, file rack, etc.).

Review of Tasks: The risk assessment team also reviewed the work tasks of our employees to determine the presence of hazards, conditions, operations, and situations that might place workers at risk of occupational assault incidents. The following factors were considered:

- exchange of money with the public
- working alone or in small numbers
- working late at night or early in the morning hours
- working in a high-crime area
- guarding valuable property or possessions
- working in community settings
- staffing levels

From this analysis, the following issues have been identified:

- Employees in client service area exchange money with clients.
- There are several employees in the shop and lab areas who work very late hours or come in very early in the morning.

WORKPLACE SURVEY

Under the direction of the risk assessment team, we distributed a survey among all of our employees to identify any additional issues that were not noted in the initial stages of the hazard assessment. From that survey, the following issues have been identified:

- Employees who work in the field have experienced threats of violence on several occasions, and there have been several near-miss incidents. Employees noted that they were unsure of how to handle the situation and that they are often afraid to travel by themselves to areas they perceive are dangerous.
- Employees who work directly with clients in the office have also experienced threats, both verbal and physical, from some of the clients.

WORKPLACE HAZARD CONTROL AND PREVENTION

In order to reduce the risk of workplace violence, the following measures have been recommended:

Engineering Controls and Building and Work Area Design

- Employees who have client contact in the facility will have their work areas designed to ensure that they are protected from possible threats from their clients.

- Changes to be completed as soon as possible include arranging desks and chairs to prevent entrapment of the employees; removing items from the top of desks, such as scissors, staplers, and so on, that can be used as weapons; and installing panic buttons to assist employees when they are threatened by clients. The buttons can be activated by one's foot. The signal will be transmitted to a supervisor's desk, as well as the security desk, which is always staffed.

Management has instituted the following as a result of the workplace security inspection and recommendations made by the risk assessment team:

- A plexiglass payment window has been installed for employees who handle money and need to take payments from clients (the number of employees who take money will be strictly limited).
- Adequate lighting systems have been installed for indoor building areas as well as areas around the outside of the facility and in the parking areas. The lighting systems will be maintained on a regular basis to ensure the safety of all employees.
- Locks have been installed on restroom doors, and keys will be given to each department. Restroom doors are to be kept locked at all times. Supervisors will ensure that the keys are returned to ensure continued security for employees in their areas.
- Panic buttons have been installed in employees' work areas.
- A memorandum has been sent to all employees requesting that they remove any items from their desks that can be used as weapons, such as scissors, staplers, and so on.

These changes were completed by **January 1, 2008.**

Policies and procedures developed as a result of the risk assessment team recommendations:

- Employees who are required to work in the field and who feel that the situation is unsafe should travel in "buddy" systems or with an escort from their supervisor.
- Employees who work in the field will report to their supervisor periodically throughout the day. They will be provided with a personal beeper or cell phone, which will allow them to contact assistance should an incident occur.
- Access to the building will be controlled. All employees have been given a name badge which is to be worn at all times. If employees come in early or are working past 7:30 p.m., they must enter and exit through the main entrance.
- Visitors will be required to sign in at the front desk. All clients must enter through the main entrance to gain access.

TRAINING AND EDUCATION

Training for all employees, including managers and supervisors, was given on **September 11, 2008**. This training will be repeated every two years. Training included:

- a review and definition of workplace violence
- a full explanation and full description of our program (all employees were given a copy of this program at orientation)

- instructions on how to report all incidents, including threats and verbal abuse
- methods of recognizing and responding to workplace security hazards
- training on how to identify potential workplace security hazards (such as no lights in parking lot while leaving late at night, unknown person loitering outside the building, etc.)
- review of measures that have been instituted in this organization to prevent workplace violence, including:
  ○ use of security equipment and procedures
  ○ how to attempt to defuse hostile or threatening situations
  ○ how to summon assistance in case of an emergency or hostage situation
- post-incident procedures, including medical follow-up and the availability of counseling and referral

Additional specialized training was given to:

- employees who work in the field
- employees who handle money with clients
- employees who work after hours or come in early

Specialized training included:

- personal safety
- importance of the buddy system
- recognizing unsafe situations and how to handle them during off hours

This training was conducted by in-house staff, with assistance from the local police department, on **October 1, 2008,** and will be repeated every two years.

Trainers were qualified and knowledgeable. Our trainers are professionals—**certified by the Society of Industrial Security.**

At the end of each training session, employees are asked to evaluate the session and make suggestions on how to improve the training.

All training records are filed with **the Human Resource Department/Personnel Department**.

Workplace violence prevention training will be given to new employees as part of their orientation.

A general review of this program will be conducted every two years. Our training program will be updated to reflect changes in our workplace prevention program.

INCIDENT REPORTING AND INVESTIGATION

All incidents must be reported within **four (4) hours**. An "Incident Report Form" will be completed for all incidents. One copy will be forwarded to the risk assessment team for their review and a copy will be filed with **the Human Resource/Personnel Department**.

Each incident will be evaluated by the risk assessment team. The team will discuss the causes of the incident and will make recommendations on how to revise the program to prevent similar incidents from occurring. All revisions of the program will be put into writing and made available to all employees.

RECORDKEEPING

We will maintain an accurate record of all workplace violence incidents. All incident report forms will be kept for a minimum of **seven (7) years**, or for the time specified in the statute of limitations for our local jurisdiction.

Any injury that requires more than first aid, is a lost-time injury, requires modified duty, or causes loss of consciousness, will be recorded on the OSHA 200 log. Doctors' reports and supervisors' reports will be kept of each recorded incident, if applicable.

Incidents of abuse, verbal attack, or aggressive behavior that may be threatening to the employee, but not resulting in injury, will be recorded. These records will be evaluated on a regular basis by the risk assessment team.

Minutes of the risk assessment team meetings shall be kept for **three (3) years**.

Records of training program contents, and the sign-in sheets of all attendees, shall be kept for **five (5) years**. Qualifications of the trainers shall be maintained along with the training records.

APPENDIX A

Special-Interest Areas

Hospitals

Today more than five million U.S. hospital workers from many occupations perform a wide variety of duties. They are exposed to many safety and health hazards, including violence. Recent data indicate that hospital workers are at high risk for experiencing violence in the workplace. According to estimates of the Bureau of Labor Statistics (BLS), 2,637 nonfatal assaults on hospital workers occurred in 1999—a rate of 8.3 assaults per 10,000 workers. This rate is much higher than the rate of nonfatal assaults for all private-sector industries, which is only 2 per 10,000 workers.

Several studies indicate that violence often takes place during times of high activity and interaction with patients, such as at mealtimes and during visiting hours and patient transportation. Assaults may occur when service is denied; when a patient is involuntarily admitted; or when a health-care worker attempts to set limits on eating, drinking, or tobacco or alcohol use.

The circumstances of hospital violence differ from the circumstances of workplace violence in general. In convenience stores and taxicabs, violence most often relates to robbery. In many other workplaces, most violence is perpetrated by customers or employees. Violence in hospitals usually results from patients and occasionally from their family members who feel frustrated, vulnerable, and out of control.

Although anyone working in a hospital may become a victim of violence, nurses and aides who have the most direct contact with patients are at higher risk. Other hospital personnel at increased risk of violence include emergency response personnel, hospital safety officers, and all health-care providers.

Violence may occur anywhere in the hospital, but it is most frequent in the following areas:

- psychiatric wards
- emergency rooms
- waiting rooms
- geriatric units

The risk factors for violence vary from hospital to hospital depending on location, size, and type of care. Common risk factors for hospital violence include the following:

- working directly with volatile people, especially if they are under the influence of drugs or alcohol or have a history of violence or certain psychotic diagnoses
- working when understaffed—especially during mealtimes and visiting hours
- transporting patients
- long waits for service
- overcrowded, uncomfortable waiting rooms
- working alone
- poor environmental design
- inadequate security
- lack of staff training and policies for preventing and managing crises with potentially volatile patients
- drug and alcohol abuse
- access to firearms
- unrestricted movement of the public
- poorly lit corridors, rooms, parking lots, and other areas

PREVENTION STRATEGIES

To prevent violence in hospitals, employers should develop a safety and health program that includes management commitment; employee participation; hazard identification; safety and health training; and hazard prevention, control, and reporting. Employers should evaluate this program periodically. Although risk factors for violence are specific for each hospital and its work scenarios, employers can follow general prevention strategies.

Environmental Design

- Develop emergency signaling, alarms, and monitoring systems.
- Install security devices such as metal detectors to prevent armed persons from entering the hospital.

- Install other security devices such as cameras and good lighting in hallways.
- Provide security escorts to the parking lots at night.
- Design waiting areas to accommodate and assist visitors and patients who may have a delay in service.
- Design the triage area and other public areas to minimize the risk of assault.
- Provide staff restrooms and emergency exits.
- Install enclosed nurses' stations.
- Install deep service counters or bullet-resistant and shatterproof glass enclosures in reception areas.
- Arrange furniture and other objects to minimize their use as weapons.

Administrative Controls

- Design staffing patterns to prevent personnel from working alone and to minimize patient waiting time.
- Restrict the movement of the public in hospitals by card-controlled access.
- Develop a system for alerting security personnel when violence is threatened.

Behavior Modifications

- Provide all workers with training in recognizing and managing assaults, resolving conflicts, and maintaining hazard awareness.

SAFETY TIPS FOR HOSPITAL WORKERS

Watch for signals that may be associated with impending violence:

- verbally expressed anger and frustration
- body language such as threatening gestures
- signs of drug or alcohol use
- presence of a weapon

Maintain behavior that helps defuse anger:

- Present a calm, caring attitude.
- Don't match the threats.
- Don't give orders.
- Acknowledge the person's feelings (for example, "I know you are frustrated").
- Avoid any behavior that may be interpreted as aggressive (for example, moving rapidly, getting too close, touching, or speaking loudly).

Be alert:

- Evaluate each situation for potential violence when you enter a room or begin to relate to a patient or visitor.
- Be vigilant throughout the encounter.
- Don't isolate yourself with a potentially violent person.
- Always keep an open path for exiting—don't let the potentially violent person stand between you and the door.

Take these steps if you can't defuse the situation quickly:

- Remove yourself from the situation.
- Call security for help.
- Report any violent incidents to your management.

All hospitals should develop a comprehensive violence prevention program. No universal strategy exists to prevent violence. The risk factors vary from hospital to hospital and from unit to unit. Hospitals should form multidisciplinary committees that include direct-care staff as well as union representatives (if available) to identify risk factors in specific work scenarios and to develop strategies for reducing them.

All hospital workers should be alert and cautious when interacting with patients and visitors. They should actively participate in safety training programs and be familiar with their employer's policies, procedures, and materials on violence prevention.

Case Reports:
Prevention Strategies That Have Worked

A security screening system in a Detroit hospital included stationary metal detectors supplemented by hand-held units. The system prevented the entry of 33 handguns, 1,324 knives, and 97 mace-type sprays during a six-month period.

A violence reporting program in the Portland, Oregon, Veterans Administration Medical Center identified patients with a history of violence in a computerized database. The program helped reduce the number of all violent attacks by 91.6 percent by alerting staff to take additional safety measures when serving these patients.

A system restricting movement of visitors in a New York City hospital used identification badges and color-coded passes to limit each visitor to a specific floor. The hospital also enforced the limit of two visitors at a time per patient. Over eighteen months, these actions reduced the number of reported violent crimes by 65 percent.

Schools

There are three major components to a comprehensive school safety plan. Failure to attend to one of these components will jeopardize the effectiveness of the others.

The school safety plan is built around the three components of an anti-violence effort: interdiction, intervention, and prevention. Each activity that a school engages in to alleviate violence is part of one or more of these components. Each component contains a constellation of programs and processes. Below is a brief explanation of these components.

1. Interdiction. This component addresses the procedures and processes necessary to prohibit and discourage acts of violence. It includes programs and practices that ensure that the school is and will remain safe. Board policy, supervision techniques, security, and a variety of management techniques are included in this component.
2. Intervention. The intervention effort recognizes that there will be pupils who are unable or unwilling to modify their behavior to conform to the school's discipline and conduct policies and regulations. Intervention efforts are remedial. These programs include counseling, peer mediation, conflict resolution, and alternative school placement, among others.
3. Prevention. This component includes the development of programs that address the causes of violent and disruptive behavior. This component encompasses curriculum and programs including mentoring programs; anger-management and -reduction programs; career-path education; and value, virtue, and justice units that are spliced into the standard curriculum.

Establishing or restoring an interdiction capability will be the initial focus for many school districts. Without a safe and orderly environment, the effectiveness of intervention and prevention strategies is compromised. If students are unable to function effectively in the school setting, intervention programs are initiated. Intervention does not make sense unless the district has met its interdiction requirement. The application of intervention programs without interdiction generates an "enabling climate," wherein the pupil is enabled to continue to be disruptive while participating in some form of intervention program. Prevention programs are the long-term solution. Prevention programs build long-term solutions and permit the pupil to make positive life choices. These programs address the cause of violence and thereby mitigate the effects.

Building the school plan

The goal of a comprehensive plan is to provide a school with a continuing capability to prevent disruptive and violent acts and cope with them if they should occur. The building of the plan is bolstered by an appreciation and use of Planning Theory and System Analysis. The plan will result in developing specific objectives and activities strengthening the capabilities of the school to prevent violence and remedy situations if necessary.

1. A school safety committee. This is a recommended vehicle for developing the school safety plan. This committee is charged with the responsibility of developing the plan and monitoring its implementation. As with any other institutional endeavor, if everyone is responsible, no one is found wanting. This committee should report on a regular basis to the board of education, administration, and school community.
2. The principal players. The framers of the plan will in many cases be the participants in plan development. The following are suggested team members.
   - The board of education. This is the policy-making and responsible group for the conduct of the school district. The board is accountable for the quality of education and for the establishment of a safe school environment. In establishing policy and regulation, it sets the tone for the school district. The board of education has a critical leadership role in the development of a proactive school safety plan.
   - The superintendent of schools. The superintendent is the CEO of the board of education. As such, he or she plays a most critical role in establishing the plan and providing the organizational support, resources, moral commitment, and supervision necessary for its success.
   - Building principals. The building principal is the individual administrator closest to the setting. The principal is aware of resources and the student population. The capabilities of personnel and resources are best assessed by this individual.
   - Teachers. The teacher is closest to the youngsters and encounters and interacts with pupils daily. The teacher delivers instruction and evaluates pupils affectively and cognitively. The teacher's quality of life and ability to perform service is determined in large measure by the security and safety of the environment.
   - Parents. The parent is a partner in the issue of school safety and antiviolence education. A holistic approach to pupil behavior must naturally consider the parent. Parents are also rightfully concerned about issues relating to their child's safety and are among the most interested stakeholders in the school community.
   - Police and law enforcement personnel. These individuals can play a most critical role in the implementation of a school's antiviolence program. Their participation in the planning process can be invaluable. Ideally, they are involved early in the plan development. The early inclusion of the po-

lice department in the planning process provides an opportunity to share ideas as well as a knowledge of roles, capabilities, and limitations.

- Security personnel. In the event that a school utilizes security personnel, it is very important to have the leadership of this group involved in the development of the plan.
- The school board attorney. Much of the ground that is covered in an anti-violence plan represents new territory. In the plan development, the attorney plays a critical role. The attorney can advise on the legality of the initiatives, propose alternatives, interpret law, and brief participants on case law and its implications to portions of the plan. The attorney can draft needed policies and regulations requisite to putting the plan into action.
- Pupil representation. Statistics indicate that the pupil is the most likely target of a violent or a personally disruptive act. The planners should seriously consider including representation from the student body in the school safety planning group. Students provide insights and perceptions into the problems that other members will not have. Due to the sensitive and secure nature of some components of the plan (critical incident planning, tactics, etc.), students' participation should be limited from time to time.
- Additional personnel and resources. Each school district is in the best position to determine what other stakeholder groups should be involved in the process of developing the plan. In addition, there are other resources that can be enlisted to assist in the plan's development. The New York State School Boards Association is an excellent resource for counsel on matters related to policy and law. Its consultants can provide assistance and direction based on experience. Other professional organizations and governmental agencies are beginning to develop capabilities to assist schools in their antiviolence efforts.

Late-Night Retail Establishments

Most workplace homicides are Type 1 violence (by strangers). For example, in California 60 percent of workplace homicides involve a person entering a small late-night retail establishment (e.g., a liquor store, a gas station, or a convenience food store) to commit a robbery. During the commission of the robbery, an employee or, more likely, the proprietor is killed or injured.

Employees or proprietors who have face-to-face contact and exchange money with the public, work late at night and into the early morning hours, and work alone or in very small numbers are at greatest risk from an assailant pretending to be a customer as a pretext to enter the establishment, but who has no legitimate business relationship to the workplace.

Late Night Retail Violence Prevention Checklist

PRE-EVENT MEASURES

Make your store unattractive to robbers by taking these measures:
- Remove clutter, obstructions, and signs from the windows so that there is an unobstructed view of the store counter and/or cash register.
- Keep the store and parking lot as brightly lit as local law allows.
- Keep an eye on what is going on outside the store and report any suspicious persons or activities to the police.
- When there are no customers in the store, keep yourself busy with other tasks away from the cash register.
- Post emergency police and fire department numbers and the store's address by the phone.
- Mount mirrors on the ceiling to help you keep an eye on hidden corners of the store. Consider surveillance cameras to record what goes on in the store and to act as a deterrent.
- Post signs that are easy to spot from the outside of the store, informing customers that you have a limited amount of cash on hand.
- Limit accessible cash to a small amount and keep only small bills in the cash register.
- Use a time access safe for larger bills and deposit them as they are received.
- Use only one register after dark and leave unused registers open with empty cash drawers tilted up for all to see.
- Let your customers know that you only keep a small amount of cash on hand.

EVENT MEASURES

- If you are robbed at gunpoint, stay calm and speak to the robber in a cooperative tone. Do not argue or fight with the robber and offer no resistance whatsoever. Hand over the money.
- *Never* pull a weapon during the event—it will only increase your chances of getting hurt.
- Always move slowly and explain each move to the robber before you make it.

POST-EVENT MEASURES

- Make no attempt to follow or chase the robber.
- Stay where you are until you are certain the robber has left the immediate area. Then lock the door of your store and call the police immediately.
- Do not touch anything the robber has handled.
- Write down everything you remember about the robber and the robbery while you wait for the police to arrive.
- Do not open the door of the store until the police arrive.

Retail robberies resulting in workplace assaults usually occur between the hours of eleven in the evening and six in the morning and are most often armed (gun or knife) robberies. In addition to employees who are classified as cashiers, many victims of late-night retail violence are supervisors or proprietors who are attacked while locking up their establishment for the night and janitors who are assaulted while cleaning the establishment after it is closed.

Other occupations/workplaces at risk include taxi drivers and security guards. In the case of taxi drivers, the pattern is similar to retail robberies. The attack is likely to involve an assailant pretending to be a bona fide passenger during the late night or early morning hours, who enters the taxicab to rob the driver of his or her fare receipts. Security guards are at risk of assault when protecting valuable property that is the object of an armed robbery.

What to Do in an Emergency

What should workers know before an emergency occurs?

- Be familiar with the worksite's emergency evacuation plan.
- Know the pathway to at least two alternative exits from every room/area at the workplace.
- Recognize the sound/signaling method of the fire/evacuation alarms.
- Know whom to contact in an emergency and how to contact them.
- Know how many desks or cubicles are between your workstation and two of the nearest exits so you can escape in the dark if necessary.
- Know where the fire/evacuation alarms are located and how to use them.
- Report damaged or malfunctioning safety systems and backup systems.

What should employers do when an emergency occurs?

- Sound appropriate alarms and instruct employees to leave the building.
- Notify police, firefighters, or other appropriate emergency personnel.
- Take a headcount of employees at designated meeting locations, and notify emergency personnel of any missing workers.

What should workers do in an emergency?

- Leave the area quickly but in an orderly manner, following the worksite's emergency evacuation plan. Go directly to the nearest fire-free and smoke-free stairwell recognizing that in some circumstances the only available exit route may contain limited amounts of smoke or fire.
- Listen carefully for instructions over the building's public address system.

- Crawl low, under the smoke, to breathe cleaner air if there is a fire. Test doors for heat before opening them by placing the back of your hand against the door so you do not burn your palm and fingers. Do not open a hot door, but find another exit route. Keep fire doors closed to slow the spread of smoke and fire.
- Avoid using elevators when evacuating a burning building.
- Report to the designated meeting place.
- Don't re-enter the building until directed by authorities.

If trapped during an emergency, what should workers do?

- Stay calm and take steps to protect yourself.
- Go to a room with an outside window, and telephone for help if possible.
- Stay where rescuers can see you and wave a light-colored cloth to attract attention.
- Open windows if possible, but be ready to shut them if smoke rushes in.
- Stuff clothing, towels, or newspapers around the cracks in doors to prevent smoke from entering your room.

APPENDIX C

Terrorism

Terrorism presents a new workplace hazard. Typically we know what the hazards of the workplace are, and we know how to protect workers against known risks. However, the hazards of terrorism are not a part of the workplace—they are unexpected and they may be unknown.

Protecting Building Environments

EVALUATE YOUR POTENTIAL AS A TERRORIST TARGET

There are facilities that historically appear more likely to be a terrorist target. These facilities may include

- airports
- power and nuclear plants
- bridges, tunnels, and other structures
- facilities that house chemical or biological agents
- government agencies and offices
- schools and educational institutions
- financial institutions
- media organizations

Some facilities are easier targets. These facilities may include

- facilities with easily accessible outdoor air inlets
- facilities easily accessible by unauthorized personnel
- facilities with unrestricted vehicle traffic

EVALUATE YOUR BUILDING'S VULNERABILITY

Preventing terrorist access to a targeted facility requires physical security of entry, storage, roof, and mechanical areas, as well as securing access to the outdoor air intakes of the building heating, ventilating, and air-conditioning (HVAC) system. The physical security of each building should be assessed, as the risk of an attack will vary considerably from building to building. While the identification and resolution of building vulnerabilities will be specific to each building, some physical security actions are applicable to many building types. The Centers for Disease Control and Prevention (CDC) and the National Institute for Occupational Safety and Health (NIOSH) have developed new guidelines for protecting buildings, and particularly ventilation systems, in commercial and government buildings from chemical, biological, and radiological attacks. These guidelines offer practical advice to building owners, managers, and maintenance staffs on the steps they can take to protect their ventilation system's airflow and filtration, system maintenance, program administration, and maintenance staff training. The guidelines recommend that security measures be adopted for air intakes and return-air grilles, and that access to building operations systems and building design information should be restricted. More information on protecting buildings can be found in *Guidance for Protecting Building Environments from Airborne Chemical, Biological, or Radiological Attacks*, NIOSH Publication #2002-139 (U.S. Centers for Disease Control and Prevention, National Institute for Occupational Safety and Health, www.cdc.gov/niosh).

BUILDING SECURITY ACTIONS

- Prevent access to outdoor air intakes.
- Prevent public access to mechanical areas.
- Prevent public access to building roof.
- Implement security measures to protect vulnerable areas.
- Isolate lobbies, mailrooms, loading docks, and storage areas.
- Restrict access to building operations systems by outside personnel.
- Restrict access to building information (design, operation, emergency plans).
- Implement general building security upgrades.

BUILDING SECURITY UPGRADES

- Install alarms, closed-circuit television, fencing, and/or security guards.
- Test the alarms monthly, and replace the alarms every ten years.
- Provide working sprinkler systems and fire extinguishers.
- Conduct employee background checks.

- Eliminate curbside parking.
- Control vehicle entrance to parking lots, or locate parking away from the building.
- Issue vehicle identification decals.
- Install building access control devices.
- Limit shipping/receiving access to approved vendors/carriers.
- Secure return-air grilles.
- Escort or pre-approve mechanical contractors for sensitive areas.
- Develop emergency response plans, policies, and procedures.
- Coordinate the plans with local emergency-response personnel.
- Train and rehearse the procedures, making sure that building operators can quickly manipulate and shut down the HVAC system.
- Determine how to seal off entrances and exits.
- Plan escape routes.
- Select an outdoor meeting place.
- Practice the escape plan.

BUILDING HVAC SYSTEM CONTROLS

In response to an air-contaminant event, it would be necessary to manipulate the HVAC system. Thus, it is important to evaluate the specific HVAC control options.

HVAC system controls

- Identify system shutdown.
- Increase outside air exchange (up to 100 percent outdoor air).
- Check zone pressurization.
- Locate local area exhaust.
- Test strategic equipment.
- Install the highest-efficiency filtration compatible with the HVAC system's design criteria.

Outdoor air intakes

- Identify and prevent unauthorized access.
- Relocate intakes to an inaccessible area.
- Build extensions to protect vulnerable intakes.
- Create a security zone around intakes.

Mechanical areas and roofs

- Restrict access to prevent tampering with or contamination of HVAC and other mechanical equipment.

- Secure mechanical and HVAC areas throughout the building.
- Require authorized roof access. Access to any mechanical area should be strictly controlled, a log of entry into the area maintained, and accountability for keys, key codes, and access cards enforced.

For buildings that are high risk

Consider installing filters or devices that capture and kill biologicals in air returns from specific areas (mailrooms, etc.) and/or outdoor air supply.
Caution:

- Do not permanently seal or restrict outdoor air intakes. The exception would be an outdoor air release of a biological, nuclear, or chemical agent. In that case it may be better to shut down the HVAC system, seal outdoor air entrances, and remain in the building. In such an emergency, use of a disposable N-95 filter respirator could be effective in reducing exposure.
- Do not modify HVAC systems, including filters, without evaluating the system effects and the effect the modifications would have on building occupants.
- Do not interfere with fire protection systems.

Emergency Plans:
What to Do in the Event of a Terrorist Attack

EXPLOSIVES

Terrorists have used explosive devices as one of their most common weapons. Terrorists do not have to look far to find out how to make explosive devices; the information is readily available in books and other information sources. The materials needed for an explosive device can be found in many places including variety, hardware, and auto supply stores. Explosive devices are highly portable, using vehicles and humans as a means of transport. They are easily detonated from remote locations or by suicide bombers.

Conventional bombs have been used to damage and destroy financial, political, social, and religious institutions. Attacks have occurred in public places and on city streets, with thousands of people around the world injured and killed.

Parcels that should make you suspicious

- are unexpected or from someone unfamiliar to you
- have no return address, or have one that can't be verified as legitimate
- are marked with restrictive endorsements such as "Personal," "Confidential," or "Do not X-ray"
- have protruding wires or aluminum foil, strange odors, or stains

- show a city or state in the postmark that doesn't match the return address
- are of unusual weight given their size, or are lopsided or oddly shaped
- are marked with threatening language
- have inappropriate or unusual labeling
- have excessive postage or packaging material, such as masking tape and string
- have misspellings of common words
- are addressed to someone no longer with your organization or are otherwise outdated
- have incorrect titles or titles without a name
- are not addressed to a specific person
- have handwritten or poorly typed addresses

If you receive a telephoned bomb threat, you should do the following:

- Get as much information from the caller as possible.
- Keep the caller on the line and record everything that is said.
- Notify the police and the building management.

During an Explosion

If there is an explosion:

- Get under a sturdy table or desk if things are falling around you. When they stop falling, leave quickly, watching for obviously weakened floors and stairways. As you exit from the building, be especially watchful of falling debris.
- Leave the building as quickly as possible. Do not stop to retrieve personal possessions or make phone calls.
- Do not use elevators.

Once you are out:

- Do not stand in front of windows, glass doors, or other potentially hazardous areas.
- Move away from sidewalks or streets to be used by emergency officials or others still exiting the building.

If you are trapped in debris:

- If possible, use a flashlight to signal your location to rescuers.
- Avoid unnecessary movement so you don't kick up dust.

- Cover your nose and mouth with anything you have on hand. (Dense-weave cotton material can act as a good filter. Try to breathe through the material.)
- Tap on a pipe or wall so rescuers can hear where you are.
- If possible, use a whistle to signal rescuers.
- Shout only as a last resort. Shouting can cause you to inhale dangerous amounts of dust.

BIOLOGICAL DANGERS

Biological agents are organisms or toxins that can kill or incapacitate people, livestock, and crops. The three basic groups of biological agents that would likely be used as weapons are bacteria, viruses, and toxins. Most biological agents are difficult to grow and maintain. Many break down quickly when exposed to sunlight and other environmental factors, while others, such as anthrax spores, are very long lived. Biological agents can be dispersed by spraying them into the air, by infecting animals that carry the disease to humans, and by contaminating food and water. Delivery methods include the following:

- Aerosols. Biological agents are dispersed into the air, forming a fine mist that may drift for miles. Inhaling the agent may cause disease in people or animals.
- Animals. Some diseases are spread by insects and animals, such as fleas, mice, flies, mosquitoes, and livestock.
- Food and water contamination. Some pathogenic organisms and toxins may persist in food and water supplies. Most microbes can be killed, and toxins deactivated, by cooking food and boiling water. Most microbes are killed by boiling water for one minute, but some require longer. Follow official instructions.
- Person-to-person spread. Humans have been the source of infection for smallpox, plague, and the Lassa viruses.

Specific information on biological agents is available at the Centers for Disease Control and Prevention's website, www.bt.cdc.gov.

INDUSTRIAL CHEMICALS: THE "TEN-STEP HAZARD ANALYSIS"

The CDC developed the "Ten-Step Hazard Analysis" to help employers identify risks posed by industrial chemicals and prevent their use as improvised weapons.

1. Identify, assess, and prioritize risks: highly hazardous chemicals, explosives, easily accessible piping and valves, railway cars of hazardous chemicals at leased sidings, and so on.

2. Identify local sources of chemicals or biologicals that may be used in improvised weapons.
3. Evaluate potential exposure pathways.
4. Identify potential acute and chronic health impacts.
5. Estimate potential impacts on infrastructure and the environment.
6. Identify health risk communication needs.
7. Identify methods to mitigate potential hazards.
8. Identify specific steps to prevent the use of industrial chemicals as improvised weapons.
9. Incorporate the risk assessment, mitigation, and prevention information into emergency response plans.
10. Conduct training exercises to prepare to prevent and mitigate the risks.

Protective Measures

BEFORE A BIOLOGICAL ATTACK

The following are guidelines for what you should do to prepare for a biological threat:

- Check with your doctor to ensure all required or suggested immunizations are up to date. Children and older adults are particularly vulnerable to biological agents.
- Consider installing a High Efficiency Particulate Air (HEPA) filter in your furnace return duct. These filters remove particles in the 0.3 to 10 micron range and will filter out most biological agents that may enter your house. If you do not have a central heating or cooling system, a stand-alone portable HEPA filter can be used.

FILTRATION IN BUILDINGS

Building owners and managers should determine the type and level of filtration in their structures and the level of protection it provides against biological agents. The National Institute of Occupational Safety and Health (NIOSH) provides technical guidance on this topic in their publication *Guidance for Filtration and Air-Cleaning Systems to Protect Building Environments from Airborne Chemical, Biological, or Radiological Attacks*.

DURING A BIOLOGICAL ATTACK

In the event of a biological attack, public health officials may not immediately be able to provide information on what you should do. It will take time to determine what the illness is, how it should be treated, and who is in danger. Watch television, listen to radio, or check the Internet for official news and information including signs and symptoms of the disease, areas in danger, if medications or vaccinations are being distributed, and where you should seek medical attention if you become ill.

The first evidence of an attack may be when you notice symptoms of the disease caused by exposure to an agent. Be suspicious of any symptoms you notice, but do not assume that any illness is a result of the attack. Use common sense and practice good hygiene.

If you become aware of an unusual and suspicious substance nearby:

- Move away quickly.
- Wash with soap and water.
- Contact authorities.
- Listen to the media for official instructions.
- Seek medical attention if you become sick.

If you are exposed to a biological agent:

- Remove and bag your clothes and personal items. Follow official instructions for disposal of contaminated items.
- Wash yourself with soap and water and put on clean clothes.
- Seek medical assistance. You may be advised to stay away from others or even quarantined.

Using HEPA Filters

HEPA filters are useful in biological attacks. If you have a central heating and cooling system in your home with a HEPA filter, leave it on if it is running or turn the fan on if it is not running. Moving the air in the house through the filter will help remove the agents from the air. If you have a portable HEPA filter, take it with you to the internal room where you are seeking shelter and turn it on.

If you are in an apartment or office building that has a modern central heating and cooling system, the system's filtration should provide a relatively safe level of protection from outside biological contaminants.

HEPA filters will not filter chemical agents.

After a Biological Attack

In some situations, such as the case of the anthrax letters sent in 2001, people may be alerted to potential exposure. If this is the case, pay close attention to all official warnings and instructions on how to proceed. The delivery of medical services for a biological event may be handled differently to respond to increased demand. The basic public health procedures and medical protocols for handling exposure to biological agents are the same as for any infectious disease. It is important for you to pay attention to official instructions via radio, television, and emergency alert systems.

CHEMICAL ATTACKS

Chemical agents are poisonous vapors, aerosols, liquids, and solids that have toxic effects on people, animals, or plants. They can be released by bombs or sprayed from aircraft, boats, and vehicles. They can be used as a liquid to create a hazard to people and the environment. Some chemical agents may be odorless and tasteless. They can have an immediate effect (a few seconds to a few minutes) or a delayed effect (two to forty-eight hours). While potentially lethal, chemical agents are difficult to deliver in lethal concentrations. Outdoors, the agents often dissipate rapidly. Chemical agents also are difficult to produce.

A chemical attack could come without warning. Signs of a chemical release include people having difficulty breathing; experiencing eye irritation; losing coordination; becoming nauseated; or having a burning sensation in the nose, throat, and lungs. Also, the presence of many dead insects or birds may indicate a chemical agent release.

Before a Chemical Attack

The following are guidelines for what you should do to prepare for a chemical attack:

- Check your disaster supplies kit to make sure it includes
  - a roll of duct tape and scissors
  - plastic for doors, windows, and vents for the room in which you will shelter in place (To save critical time during an emergency, pre-measure and cut the plastic sheeting for each opening.)
- Choose an internal room to shelter, preferably one without windows and on the highest level.

During a Chemical Attack

The following are guidelines for what you should do in a chemical attack.
If you are instructed to remain in your home or office building:

- Close doors and windows and turn off all ventilation, including furnaces, air conditioners, vents, and fans.
- Seek shelter in an internal room and take your disaster supplies kit.
- Seal the room with duct tape and plastic sheeting.
- Listen to your radio for instructions from authorities.

If you are caught in or near a contaminated area:

- Move away immediately in a direction upwind of the source.
- Find shelter as quickly as possible.

After a Chemical Attack

Decontamination is needed within minutes of exposure to minimize health consequences. Do not leave the safety of a shelter to go outdoors to help others until authorities announce it is safe to do so.

A person affected by a chemical agent requires immediate medical attention from a professional. If medical help is not immediately available, decontaminate yourself and assist in decontaminating others.

Decontamination guidelines are as follows:

- Use extreme caution when helping others who have been exposed to chemical agents.
- Remove all clothing and other items in contact with the body. Contaminated clothing normally removed over the head should be cut off to avoid contact with the eyes, nose, and mouth. Put contaminated clothing and items into a plastic bag and seal it. Decontaminate hands using soap and water. Remove eyeglasses or contact lenses. Put glasses in a pan of household bleach to decontaminate them, and then rinse and dry.
- Flush eyes with water.
- Gently wash face and hair with soap and water before thoroughly rinsing with water.
- Decontaminate other body areas likely to have been contaminated. Blot (do not swab or scrape) with a cloth soaked in soapy water and rinse with clear water.
- Change into uncontaminated clothes. Clothing stored in drawers or closets is likely to be uncontaminated.
- Proceed to a medical facility for screening and professional treatment.

NUCLEAR BLAST

A nuclear blast is an explosion with intense light and heat, a damaging pressure wave, and widespread radioactive material that can contaminate the air, water, and ground surfaces for miles around. A nuclear device can range from a weapon carried by an intercontinental missile launched by a hostile nation or terrorist organization, to a small portable nuclear device transported by an individual. All nuclear devices cause deadly effects when exploded, including blinding light, intense heat (thermal radiation), initial nuclear radiation, blast, fires started by the heat pulse, and secondary fires caused by the destruction.

Hazards of Nuclear Devices

The extent, nature, and arrival time of these hazards are difficult to predict. The geographical dispersion of hazard effects will be defined by the following:

- Size of the device. A more powerful bomb will produce more distant effects.
- Height above the ground the device was detonated. This will determine the extent of blast effects.
- Nature of the surface beneath the explosion. Some materials are more likely to become radioactive and airborne than others. Flat areas are more susceptible to blast effects.
- Existing meteorological conditions. Wind speed and direction will affect arrival time of fallout; precipitation may wash fallout from the atmosphere.

Radioactive Fallout

Even if individuals are not close enough to the nuclear blast to be affected by the direct impacts, they may be affected by radioactive fallout. Any nuclear blast results in some fallout. Blasts that occur near the earth's surface create much greater amounts of fallout than blasts that occur at higher altitudes. This is because the tremendous heat produced from a nuclear blast causes an updraft of air that forms the familiar mushroom cloud. When a blast occurs near the earth's surface, millions of vaporized dirt particles also are drawn into the cloud. As the heat diminishes, radioactive materials that have vaporized condense on the particles and fall back to earth. The phenomenon is called radioactive fallout. This fallout material decays over a long period of time, and is the main source of residual nuclear radiation.

Fallout from a nuclear explosion may be carried by wind currents for hundreds of miles if the right conditions exist. Effects from even a small portable device exploded at ground level can be potentially deadly.

Nuclear radiation cannot be seen, smelled, or otherwise detected by normal senses. Radiation can only be detected by radiation monitoring devices. This makes radiological emergencies different from other types of emergencies, such as floods or hurricanes. Monitoring can project the fallout arrival times, which will be announced through official warning channels. However, any increase in surface buildup of gritty dust and dirt should be a warning for taking protective measures.

Electromagnetic Pulse

In addition to other effects, a nuclear weapon detonated in or above the earth's atmosphere can create an electromagnetic pulse (EMP), a high-density electrical field. An EMP acts like a stroke of lightning but is stronger, faster, and shorter. An EMP can seriously damage electronic devices connected to power sources or antennas. This includes communication systems, computers, electrical appliances, and automobile or aircraft ignition systems. The damage could range from a minor interruption to actual burnout of components. Most electronic equipment within 1,000 miles of a high-altitude nuclear detonation could be affected. Battery-powered radios with short antennas generally would not be affected. Although an EMP is unlikely to harm most people, it could harm those with pacemakers or other implanted electronic devices.

Protection from a Nuclear Blast

The danger of a massive strategic nuclear attack on the United States is predicted by experts to be less likely today. However, terrorism, by nature, is unpredictable.

If there were risk of an attack, people living near potential targets could be advised to evacuate or they could decide on their own to evacuate to an area not considered a likely target. Protection from radioactive fallout would require taking shelter in an underground area or in the middle of a large building.

In general, potential targets include

- strategic missile sites and military bases
- centers of government such as Washington, D.C., and state capitals
- important transportation and communication centers
- manufacturing, industrial, technology, and financial centers
- petroleum refineries, electrical power plants, and chemical plants
- major ports and airfields

The three factors for protecting oneself from radiation and fallout are distance, shielding, and time.

- Distance. The more distance between you and the fallout particles, the better. An underground area such as a home or office building basement offers more protection than the first floor of a building. A floor near the middle of a high-rise may be better, depending on what is nearby at that level on which significant fallout particles would collect. Flat roofs collect fallout particles, so the top floor is not a good choice; nor is a floor adjacent to a neighboring flat roof.
- Shielding. The heavier and denser the materials—thick walls, concrete, bricks, books, and earth—between you and the fallout particles, the better.
- Time. Fallout radiation loses its intensity fairly rapidly. In time, you will be able to leave the fallout shelter. Radioactive fallout poses the greatest danger to people during the first two weeks, by which time it has declined to about 1 percent of its initial radiation level.

Remember that any protection, however temporary, is better than none at all, and the more shielding, distance, and time you can take advantage of, the better.

Before a Nuclear Blast

To prepare for a nuclear blast, you should do the following:

- Find out from officials if any public buildings in your community have been designated as fallout shelters. If none have been designated, make your own list of potential shelters near your home, workplace, and school. These places would include basements or the windowless center area of middle floors in high-rise buildings, as well as subways and tunnels.
- If you live in an apartment building or high-rise, talk to the manager about the safest place in the building for sheltering and about providing for building occupants until it is safe to go out.
- During periods of increased risk, augment your disaster supplies to be adequate for up to two weeks.

Taking shelter during a nuclear blast is absolutely necessary. There are two kinds of shelters, blast and fallout:

- Blast shelters are specifically constructed to offer some protection against blast pressure, initial radiation, heat, and fire. But even a blast shelter cannot withstand a direct hit from a nuclear explosion.
- Fallout shelters do not need to be specially constructed for protecting against fallout. They can be any protected space, provided that the walls and roof are thick and dense enough to absorb the radiation given off by fallout particles.

During a Nuclear Blast

The following are guidelines for what to do in the event of a nuclear explosion. If an attack warning is issued:

- Take cover as quickly as you can, below ground if possible, and stay there until instructed to do otherwise.
- Listen for official information and follow instructions.

If you are caught outside and unable to get inside immediately:

- Do not look at the flash or fireball—it can blind you.
- Take cover behind anything that might offer protection.

- Lie flat on the ground and cover your head. If the explosion is some distance away, it could take 30 seconds or more for the blast wave to hit.
- Take shelter as soon as you can, even if you are many miles from ground zero where the attack occurred. Radioactive fallout can be carried by the winds for hundreds of miles. Remember the three protective factors: distance, shielding, and time.

After a Nuclear Blast

Decay rates of the radioactive fallout are the same for any size nuclear device. However, the amount of fallout will vary based on the size of the device and its proximity to the ground. Therefore, it might be necessary for those in the areas with highest radiation levels to shelter for up to a month.

The heaviest fallout would be limited to the area at or downwind from the explosion, and 80 percent of the fallout would occur during the first twenty-four hours.

People in most of the areas that would be affected could be allowed to come out of shelter within a few days and, if necessary, evacuate to unaffected areas.

Returning to Your Home

Remember the following:

- Keep listening to the radio and television for news about what to do, where to go, and places to avoid.
- Stay away from damaged areas. Stay away from areas marked "radiation hazard" or "HAZMAT." Remember that radiation cannot be seen, smelled, or otherwise detected by human senses.

Radiological Dispersion Device

Terrorist use of an radiological dispersion device (RDD) — often called "dirty nuke" or "dirty bomb"—is considered far more likely than use of a nuclear explosive device. An RDD combines a conventional explosive device—such as a bomb—with radioactive material. It is designed to scatter dangerous and sublethal amounts of radioactive material over a general area. Such RDDs appeal to terrorists because they require limited technical knowledge to build and deploy compared to a nuclear device. Also, the radioactive materials in RDDs are widely used in medicine, agriculture, industry, and research, and are easier to obtain than weapons-grade uranium or plutonium.

The primary purpose of terrorist use of an RDD is to cause psychological fear and economic disruption. Some devices could cause fatalities from exposure to radioactive materials. Depending on the speed at which the area of the RDD detonation was evacuated or how successful people were at sheltering-in-place, the number of deaths and injuries from an RDD might not be substantially greater than from a conventional bomb explosion.

The size of the affected area and the level of destruction caused by an RDD would depend on the sophistication and size of the conventional bomb, the type of radioactive material used, the quality and quantity of the radioactive material, and the local meteorological conditions—primarily wind and precipitation. The area affected could be placed off-limits to the public for several months during cleanup efforts.

Before an RDD Event

There is no way of knowing how much warning time there will be before an attack by terrorists using an RDD, so being prepared in advance and knowing what to do and when is important. Take the same protective measures you would for fallout resulting from a nuclear blast.

During an RDD Event

While the explosive blast will be immediately obvious, the presence of radiation will not be known until trained personnel with specialized equipment are on the scene. Whether you are indoors or outdoors, at home or at work, be extra cautious. It would be safer to assume radiological contamination has occurred—particularly in an urban setting or near other likely terrorist targets—and take the proper precautions. As with any radiation, you want to avoid or limit exposure. This is particularly true of inhaling radioactive dust that results from the explosion. As you seek shelter from any location (indoors or outdoors), if there is visual dust or other contaminants in the air, breathe though the cloth of your shirt or coat to limit your exposure. If you manage to avoid breathing radioactive dust, your proximity to the radioactive particles may still result in some radiation exposure.

If the explosion or radiological release occurs inside, get out immediately and seek safe shelter. See table C.1 for options if this is not possible.

After an RDD Event

After finding safe shelter, those who may have been exposed to radioactive material should decontaminate themselves. To do this, remove and bag your clothing (and isolate the bag away from you and others), and shower thoroughly with soap and water. Seek medical attention after officials indicate it is safe to leave shelter.

Contamination from an RDD event could affect a wide area, depending on the amount of conventional explosives used, the quantity and type of radioactive material released, and meteorological conditions. Thus, radiation dissipation

Table C.1. Emergency action in case of radiological release

Outdoors	Indoors
Seek shelter indoors immediately in the nearest undamaged building.	If you have time, turn off ventilation and heating systems, close windows, vents, fireplace dampers, exhaust fans, and clothes dryer vents. Retrieve your disaster supplies kit and a battery-powered radio and take them to your shelter room.
If appropriate shelter is not available, move as rapidly as is safe upwind and away from the location of the explosive blast. Then, seek appropriate shelter as soon as possible.	Seek shelter immediately, preferably underground or in an interior room of a building, placing as much distance and dense shielding as possible between you and the outdoors where the radioactive material may be.
Listen for official instructions and follow directions.	Seal windows and external doors that do not fit snugly with duct tape to reduce infiltration of radioactive particles. Plastic sheeting will not provide shielding from radioactivity nor from blast effects of a nearby explosion.
	Listen for official instructions and follow directions.

rates vary, but radiation from an RDD will likely take longer to dissipate due to a potentially larger localized concentration of radioactive material.

Follow these additional guidelines after an RDD event:

- Continue listening to your radio or watch the television for instructions from local officials, whether you have evacuated or sheltered in place.
- Do not return to or visit an RDD incident location for any reason.

Terrorism Knowledge Check

1. What would you do, if you were at work and
   - There was an explosion in the building?
   - You received a package in the mail that you considered suspicious?
   - You received a telephone call that was a bomb threat?
2. If caught outside during a nuclear blast, what should you do?
3. What are the three key factors for protection from nuclear blast and fallout?
4. If you take shelter in your own home, what kind of room would be safest during a chemical or biological attack?
5. In case of a chemical attack, what extra items should you have in your disaster supplies kit?

Color-Coded Risk Levels: Checklist for Individuals

GREEN = LOW RISK

- Develop a family emergency plan. Share it with family and friends, and practice the plan. Visit www.Ready.gov for help creating a plan.
- Create an emergency supply kit for your household.
- Be informed. Visit www.Ready.gov or obtain a copy of "Preparing Makes Sense, Get Ready Now" by calling 1-800-BE-READY.
- Know where to shelter and how to turn off utilities (power, gas, and water) to your home.
- Examine volunteer opportunities in your community, such as Citizen Corps, Volunteers in Police Service, Neighborhood Watch, or others, and donate your time. Consider completing an American Red Cross first aid or CPR course, or Community Emergency Response Team (CERT) course.

BLUE = GUARDED RISK

- Complete recommended steps at level green.
- Review stored disaster supplies and replace items that are outdated.
- Be alert to suspicious activity and report it to proper authorities.

YELLOW = ELEVATED RISK

- Complete recommended steps at levels green and blue.
- Ensure disaster supplies are stocked and ready.
- Check telephone numbers in family emergency plan and update as necessary.
- Develop alternate routes to/from work or school and practice them.
- Continue to be alert for suspicious activity and report it to authorities.

ORANGE = HIGH RISK

- Complete recommended steps at lower levels.
- Exercise caution when traveling. Pay attention to travel advisories.
- Review your family emergency plan and make sure all family members know what to do.
- Be patient. Expect some delays, baggage searches, and restrictions at public buildings.
- Check on neighbors or others that might need assistance in an emergency.

RED = SEVERE RISK

- Complete all recommended actions at lower levels.
- Listen to local emergency management officials.

- Stay tuned to TV or radio for current information/instructions.
- Be prepared to shelter or evacuate, as instructed.
- Expect traffic delays and restrictions.
- Provide volunteer services only as requested.
- Contact your school/business to determine status of workday.

APPENDIX D

Bomb Threat Procedures

What people are most afraid of is biological, chemical, or nuclear terrorism. However, if we consider Europe's experience, the most likely terrorism tool is a conventional bomb. This is because explosives are relatively easy to obtain and use. Schools have been the frequent targets of bomb threats. Thus, we are including the following bomb threat procedures and bomb threat checklist.

Sample Bomb Threat Procedure

1. The person receiving the call uses the checklist, notes all vital information, and reports to the site supervisor immediately.
2. The site supervisor calls 911.
3. If a bomb may be inside the building, follow these steps:
   - Check evacuation routes and evacuation area for unusual objects, which may be a bomb. Do not touch anything that may be a bomb.
   - Order evacuation. Announce the evacuation by an adult runner. Do not use intercoms, telephones, cell phones, handheld radios, pagers, bells, or other electronic devices.
   - When evacuating, check visually for unusual objects (which may be a bomb) or anything not recognized as belonging in the surrounding area. Report anything unusual to the authorities, but do not touch anything that may be a bomb.
   - Leave the lights on and the doors unlocked.
   - Move to an evacuation area well away from the building. This could be a nearby open space, such as a park, or a neighboring facility. Do not evacuate to any area where a bomb could be hidden (e.g., the parking lot) or near any object in which a bomb could be hidden (e.g., a dumpster).

- Allow law enforcement or the bomb squad to determine an "all clear," and return to work.

Sample Bomb Threat Checklist

1. Record the exact wording of the threat. _____

_____

2. Ask questions like the following:
   - When is the bomb going to go off? _____
   - Where is the bomb? _____
   - What does the bomb look like? _____
   - What kind of a bomb is it? _____
   - What will make the bomb explode? _____
   - Did you place the bomb? _____
   - Why? _____
   - Who are you? _____
   - Where do you live? _____
3. List:
   - anything that would help to identify the caller: voice type _____; nasal _____; soft _____; loud _____; slurred _____; male _____; female _____; accent _____; lisp _____
   - any background noises: street noise _____; factory _____; house noises _____; children's voices _____; PA systems _____; _____
4. Language used:
   - educated _____; incoherent _____; message read by caller _____; irrational _____; taped _____; foul _____
5. Signature of person taking the call: _____
6. Phone number that received the call: _____
7. Date and time of call: _____

APPENDIX E

Physical Security

In Step 3 we looked in general at physical security measures that can be incorporated as part of a good prevention program. The following is a more detailed explanation of what is available and how it can be implemented.

Access Controls

LOCK AND KEY SYSTEMS

Key locks consist of, but are not limited to, the following:

- Cylindrical locksets are often called key-in-knob or key-in-lever locks. They are normally used to secure offices and storerooms. The locking cylinder located in the center of the doorknob distinguishes these locks. Some cylindrical locksets have keyways in each of the opposing knobs and require a key on either side to lock and unlock them. Others unlock with a key, but may be locked by pushing or rotating a button on the inside knob. These locks are suitable only for very low-security applications. Using these locks may require compensatory measures in the form of additional locks on containers within the room.
- Dead-bolt locks are sometimes called tubular dead bolts. They are mounted on the door in a manner similar to cylindrical locksets. The primary difference is in the bolt. When the bolt is extended (locked), the dead bolt projects into the door frame at least one inch, and it cannot be forced back (unlocked) by applying pressure to the end of the bolt. The dead-bolt lock has the potential for providing acceptable levels of protection for storerooms and other areas

where more security is desired. It is recommended for use in military housing as an effective security measure in the installation's crime-prevention program. In situations where there is a window in or adjacent to the door, a double cylinder dead-bolt lock (one that requires a key to open from either side) should be used.

- Mortise locks are so named because the lock case is mortised or recessed into the edge of the door. The most common variety of mortise locks has a doorknob on each side of the door. Entrance doors often have an exterior thumb latch rather than a doorknob. The mortise lock can be locked from inside by means of a thumb turn or by a button. Mortise locks are considered low-security devices because they weaken the door in the mortised area.
- Drop-bolt locks (often referred to as jimmy-proof locks) are normally used as auxiliary locks similar to dead bolts. Both the drop-bolt lock body and the strike have interlocking leaves similar to a door hinge. When closed, locking pins in the lock body drop down into the holes provided in the strike and secure the locking system. Because the lock body and the strike are interconnected with locking pins when closed, the lock essentially becomes a single unit and is extremely difficult to separate.
- Rim-cylinder locks are mounted to the door's inside surface and are secured by screws in the door face. These locks are generally used with drop-bolt and other surface-mounted locks and latches. They consist of an outer barrel, a cylinder and ring, a tailpiece, a back mounting plate, and two mounting screws. The tailpiece screws are usually scored so that the lock can be tailored to fit varying door thicknesses.
- Unit locks are ideal in heavily traveled facilities (such as hospitals or institutional buildings). These locks are a complete, one-piece unit that slides into a notch cut into the door's latch edge. The one-size cutout of the door edge simplifies the door preparation for the lock.
- Mechanical, push-button combination locks are digital (push buttons numbered 1 through 9) combination door-locking devices used to deny area access to any individual not authorized or cleared for a specific area. These locks are normally used for access control and should be backed up by door-locking devices when the facility is unoccupied.
- Padlocks are detachable locks that are typically used with a hasp. Low-security padlocks, sometimes called secondary padlocks, are used to deter unauthorized access, and they provide only minimal resistance to force. Low-security locks are made with hardened steel shackles. Precautions must be taken to avoid confusing these locks with similar brass or bronze locks. The brass or bronze locks are commonly used but do not meet the security requirements of the hardened-shackle locks. High-security padlocks provide the maximum resistance to unauthorized entry when used with a high-security hasp.

Combination locks are available as padlocks or as mounted locks. They are low-security padlocks with combinations that are either fixed or changeable.

ACCESS BARRIERS

Turnstiles and revolving doors are access barriers that can be installed to continuously control and monitor every individual entering and or exiting a building. Whereas revolving doors are most often deployed to control the entry to a building from the street, turnstiles are usually set within the lobby of a building.

ELECTRONIC ENTRY CONTROL

The function of an entry control system is to ensure that only authorized personnel are permitted into or out of a controlled area. Entry can be controlled by locked fence gates, locked doors to a building or rooms within a building, or specially designed portals. Devices include swipe cards and key pads.

Proximity cards contain an embedded antenna that sends out a low-level fixed radio frequency signal. They can be used to open secured doors and turnstiles. The disadvantage is that possession of the card does not guarantee that it is being used by the person it was assigned to.

IDENTIFICATION SYSTEMS

An ID system provides a method of identifying personnel. The system provides for personal recognition and the use of security ID cards or badges to aid in the control and movement of personnel activities.

Standard ID cards are generally acceptable for access into areas that are unrestricted and have no security interest. Personnel requiring access to restricted areas should be issued a security ID card or badge.

Four of the most commonly used access-control ID methods are the personal recognition system, the single card or badge system, the card or badge exchange system, and the multiple card or badge system.

Personal Recognition System

The personal recognition system is the simplest of all systems. A member of the security force providing access control visually checks the person requesting entry. Entry is granted based on the following:

- The individual is recognized.
- The need to enter has been established.
- The person is on an access-control roster.

Single Card or Badge System

This system reflects permission to enter specific areas by depicting specific letters, numbers, or colors on the badge. This system lends to comparatively loose control and is not recommended for high-security areas. Permission to enter specific areas does not always go with the need to know. Because the ID cards/badges frequently remain in the bearer's possession while off duty, it affords the opportunity for alteration or duplication.

Card or Badge Exchange System

In this system, two cards/badges contain identical photographs. Each card/badge has a different background color, or one card/badge has an overprint. One card/badge is presented at the entrance to a specific area and exchanged for the second card/badge, which is worn or carried while in that area. Individual possession of the second card/badge occurs only while the bearer is in the area for which it was issued. When leaving the area, the second card/badge is returned and maintained in the security area. This method provides a greater degree of security and decreases the possibility of forgery, alteration, or duplication of the card/badge.

Multiple Card or Badge System

This system provides the greatest degree of security. Instead of having specific markings on the cards/badges denoting permission to enter various restricted areas, the multiple card/badge system makes an exchange at the entrance to each security area. The card/badge information is identical and allows for comparisons. Exchange cards/badges are maintained at each area only for individuals who have access to the specific area.

MECHANIZED/AUTOMATED SYSTEMS

An alternative to using security personnel to visually check cards/badges and access rosters is to use building card access systems or biometric access readers. These systems can control the flow of personnel entering and exiting a complex. Included in these systems are

- coded devices such as mechanical or electronic keypads or combination locks
- credential devices such as magnetic strip or proximity card readers
- biometric devices such as fingerprint readers or retina scanners

Access control and ID systems base their judgment factor on a remote capability through a routine discriminating device for positive ID. These systems do not require security staff at entry points; they identify an individual in the following manner:

- The system receives physical ID data from an individual.
- The data is encoded and compared to stored information.
- The system determines whether access is authorized.
- The information is translated into readable results.

Specialized mechanical systems are ideal for highly sensitive situations because they use a controlled process in a controlled environment to establish the required database and accuracy. One innovative technique applied to ID and admittance procedures involves dimension comparisons. The dimension of a person's full hand is compared to previously stored data to determine entry authorization. Other specialized machine readers can scan a single fingerprint or an eye retina and provide positive ID of anyone attempting entry.

An all-inclusive automated ID and access control system reinforces the security in-depth ring through its easy and rapid change capability. The computer is able to do this through its memory. Changes can be made quickly by the system's administrator.

The commercial security market has a wide range of mechanized and automated hardware and software systems. Automated equipment is chosen only after considering the security needs and the environment in which it operates. These considerations include whether the equipment is outdoors or indoors, the temperature range, and weather conditions. Assessment of security needs and the use of planning, programming, and budgeting procedures greatly assist a security manager in improving the security posture.

CARD/BADGE SPECIFICATIONS

Upon issuing a card/badge, security personnel must explain to the bearer its use and the authorizations allowed with the card/badge. This includes

- designation of the areas where an ID card/badge is required
- a description of the type of card/badge in use and the authorizations and limitations placed on the bearer
- the required presentation of the card/badge when entering or leaving each area during all hours of the day
- details of when, where, and how the card/badge should be worn, displayed, or carried
- procedures to follow in case of loss or damage of the card
- the disposition of the card/badge upon termination of employment, investigations, or personnel actions
- prerequisites for reissuing the card/badge

VISITOR IDS AND CONTROLS

Procedures must be implemented to properly identify and control personnel. This includes visitors presenting their cards/badges to security at entrances of restricted areas. Visitors are required to stay with their assigned escort. Security must ensure that visitors stay in areas relating to their visit; an uncontrolled visitor, although conspicuously identified, could acquire information for which he is not authorized.

Physical security precautions against pilferage, espionage, and sabotage require the screening, ID, and control of visitors. Visitors are generally classed in the following categories:

- persons with whom every installation or facility has business (such as suppliers, customers, insurance inspectors, and government inspectors).
- individuals or groups who desire to visit an installation or facility for personal or educational reasons (Such visits may be desired by educational, technical, or scientific organizations.)
- individuals or groups specifically sponsored by the government (such as foreign nationals visiting under technical cooperation programs and similar visits by U.S. nationals)
- guided tours to selected portions of the installation in the interest of public relations

The ID and control mechanisms for visitors must be in place. They may include the following:

- Methods of establishing the authority for admitting visitors and any limitations relative to access.
- Positive ID of visitors by personal recognition, visitor permit, or other identifying credentials. Contact the employer, supervisor, or officer in charge to validate the visit.
- The use of visitor registration forms. These forms provide a record of the visitor and the time, location, and duration of the visit.
- The use of visitor ID cards/badges. The cards/badges bear serial numbers, the area or areas to which access is authorized, the bearer's name, and escort requirements.

SMART CARDS

Smart cards, about the size and shape of a credit card, are used in access control systems to verify that the cardholder is the person he or she claims to be. They are increasingly used in one-to-one verification applications that compare a user's biometric (commonly a fingerprint or hand geometry) to the biometric template stored on the smart card.

Biometric Access Controls

Biometrics are automated methods for recognizing a person based on a physiological or behavioral characteristic. Methods most commonly used are the following:

Fingerprint scan technology (also known as fingerprint recognition) uses the impressions made by the unique, minute ridge formations or patterns found on the fingertips. Although fingerprint patterns may be similar, no two fingerprints have ever been found to contain identical individual ridge characteristics.

Hand (or finger) geometry is based on the premise that each individual's hands, although changing over time, remain characteristically the same. The technology collects over ninety automated measurements of many dimensions of the hand and fingers, using such metrics as the height of the fingers, distance between joints, and shape of the knuckles.

Retina scan technology is based on the patterns of blood vessels on the retina, a thin nerve about one-fiftieth of an inch thick located on the back of the eye. These patterns are unique from person to person. No two retinas are alike, not even in identical twins. Retinal patterns remain constant throughout a person's lifetime except in cases of certain diseases.

Iris scan technology is based on the unique visible characteristics of the eye's iris, the colored ring that surrounds the pupil. The iris of each eye is different; even identical twins have different iris patterns. The iris remains constant over a person's lifetime. Even medical procedures such as refractive surgery, cataract surgery, and cornea transplants do not change the iris's characteristics.

Facial recognition is a biometric technology that identifies people based on their facial features. Systems using this technology capture facial images from video cameras and generate templates for comparing a live facial scan of an individual to a stored template.

Speaker verification works by creating a voice template based on the unique characteristics of an individual's vocal tract, which results in differences in the cadence, pitch, and tone of voice.

Signature recognition authenticates the identity of individuals by measuring their handwritten signatures. The signature is treated as a series of movements that contain unique biometric data, such as personal rhythm, acceleration, and pressure flow.

Duress Code

The duress code is designed to protect nonsecurity personnel. If people see something suspicious, they must be trained to alert the proper authorities and not try to intervene themselves, which could put them and others in danger. For instance, a teacher who sees a stranger armed with a gun in the parking lot should not try to tackle the person but should use the duress code to summon help as quickly as possible.

The duress code is a simple word or phrase used during normal conversation to alert other security personnel that an authorized person is under duress. A duress code requires planning and rehearsal to ensure an appropriate response. This code is changed frequently to minimize compromise.

Two-Person Rule

The two-person rule is applied in many other aspects of physical security operations, such as the following:

- when uncontrolled access to vital machinery, equipment, or materiel might provide opportunity for intentional or unintentional damage that could affect the installation's mission or operation
- when uncontrolled access to funds could provide opportunity for diversion by falsification of accounts
- when uncontrolled delivery or receipt for materials could provide opportunity for pilferage through "short" deliveries and false receipts
- when access to a sensitive area could provide an opportunity for theft (Keys should be issued so that at least two people must be present to unlock the locks.)

More examples of measures an organization can take to improve security for its employees can be found in publications by the Federal Protective Service, National Institute for Occupational Safety and Health, and the Occupational Safety and Health Administration.

APPENDIX F

Legal Issues

To some extent, the law puts conflicting pressures on employers and others concerned with preventing or mitigating workplace violence. On the one hand, businesses are under a variety of legal obligations to safeguard their employees' well-being and security. Occupational safety laws impose a general requirement to maintain a safe workplace, which embraces safety from violence. For example, the Occupational Safety and Health (OSH) Act of 1970 created the Occupational Safety and Health Administration (OSHA) within the Department of Labor and encouraged employers and employees to reduce workplace hazards and to implement safety and health programs. An employer is obligated to furnish each of its employees a place of employment that is free from recognized hazards that are causing or are likely to cause death and/or serious physical harm to its employees. This includes an obligation to prevent workplace violence.

Workers' compensation laws, similarly, make employers responsible for job-related injuries. Civil rights laws require employers to protect employees against various forms of harassment, including threats or violence. In addition, employers may face civil liability after a workplace violence incident on a number of grounds—if there was negligence in hiring or retaining a dangerous person, for example, or a failure to provide proper supervision, training, or physical safety measures.

At the same time, the law requires employers to safeguard due process and other employee rights. Privacy, antidefamation, and antidiscrimination laws may limit an employer's ability to find out about the background of a present or prospective employee. The possibility of a wrongful termination lawsuit can make a company reluctant to fire someone even when there is evidence that the person may be dangerous, and can make the process a long, difficult struggle if the company does decide to seek termination. Even the Americans with Disabilities Act can sometimes pose obstacles in dealing with a potentially violent employee. Employee rights and workplace safety concerns can also collide over such issues as whether and when a worker can be compelled to get counseling or treatment as a condition of keeping his or her job.

To a large degree, these dilemmas mirror the inherent tension in a legal system with dual objectives: protecting the general good, while also protecting individual rights. Just as in every other legal field, workplace safety law has to strike a balance between those two purposes. None of the participants at the FBI's 2004 NCAVC Symposium questioned the principles of respecting due process and workers' rights or the need to balance safety precautions and antiviolence policies against appropriate privacy protection. The issue is where the boundary should be drawn.

One area where symposium participants expressed considerable concern was the restrictive effect of potential civil liability on disseminating information about employees with records of past violence or other troubling behavior on the job. Those restrictions can significantly limit the employer's ability either to screen out dangerous people before hiring, or to obtain information that would be highly relevant in a threat assessment when an incident has occurred.

For example, though rules vary somewhat from one jurisdiction to another, law enforcement agencies are ordinarily not allowed to disclose criminal records or inform employers if a worker or job applicant has been convicted of a violent crime—this even though the conviction was a matter of public record. Similarly, strict confidentiality rules shield medical and mental health records that can also have direct relevance to assessing the risk of violent behavior.

Legal considerations also inhibit the exchange of information among employers. In some cases where a company has negotiated the termination of an employee who it felt was dangerous, the settlement includes a confidentiality clause barring the company from disclosing the employee's conduct to anyone else—including to another company that may be considering the person for employment. (At times the settlement may even require purging all reports of misconduct from the company's own records.) Even where there is no confidentiality agreement, concern over liability for defamation or privacy infringement can make employers hesitant to warn others about a possibly dangerous past or present employee.

In reality, damaging but truthful information can often be disclosed without significant legal risk. But in today's litigious climate, executives and legal advisers too often tend to conclude that saying nothing is the safest course. As a result, human resources officials frequently resort to a kind of coded communication to alert a prospective employer of potential problems. Some companies ask terminated employees to sign a waiver allowing the release of information to a new or prospective employer. If the employee refuses to sign, disclosing the refusal to the new employer can also serve as a warning sign. Or the message may be sent by a no-comment response: "We are not at liberty to say anything about that person at this time."

These oblique, wink-and-nod warnings no doubt help companies avoid hiring some problem applicants. But coded messages are a poor substitute for solid, clear, factual information when an employee or applicant may be a danger to coworkers.

Helpful changes would include the following:

- standardizing guidelines so that employers will know when and how they can warn others about an employee's record of threats or violence
- modifying the restrictions on law enforcement agencies so they can release relevant criminal record information when someone appears to pose a significant danger to fellow workers
- considering ways to give companies carefully drawn exemption from liability for disclosing damaging information if it is accurate and disclosed in a good-faith effort to help protect other employees' safety
- reassessing confidentiality requirements for medical and mental health histories and determining when warnings of potential violent conduct may be appropriate
- clarifying guidelines for when and how a dangerous or potentially dangerous employee can be required to undergo mental health evaluation, counseling, or treatment

Meanwhile, within existing legal boundaries, awareness and education programs can help executives, managers, human resources officials, and legal advisers understand what is permissible, and when and how they can share information that may help avoid a violent incident. Similarly, employees can be trained in formulating antiviolence policies and disciplinary procedures that will meet due process standards while effectively protecting workplace safety.

(Excerpted from the FBI's report *Workplace Violence*.)

APPENDIX G

Violence Prevention Resources

Government Resources

Office of Personnel Management (OPM)
Employee Relations and Health Services Center
1900 E Street NW
Washington, DC 20415
(202) 606-2920

OPM's Employee Relations and Health Services Center provides advice and assistance to federal agencies on issues relating to employee relations and Employee Assistance Program policy, including workplace violence, traumatic incidents, reasonable accommodation, and discipline. OPM publications (available through the OPM rider system) include

- *A Manager's Handbook: Handling Traumatic Events*
- *Significant Cases*, a bimonthly summary of important decisions of the courts, the U.S. Merit Systems Protection Board, and the Federal Labor Relations Authority
- *New Developments in Employee and Labor Relations*, a bimonthly publication that highlights current case law, issues, and events in employee and labor relations
- *Alternative Dispute Resolution: A Resource Guide* (available by calling the phone number listed above)

Department of Health and Human Services (DHHS)
Centers for Disease Control and Prevention (CDC)

National Institute for Occupational Safety and Health (NIOSH)
Robert A. Taft Laboratories
4676 Columbia Parkway
Cincinnati, OH 45226-1998
(800) 356-4674

NIOSH has issued a publication on workplace violence, *Violence in the Workplace: Risk Factors and Prevention Strategies*, NIOSH Current Intelligence Bulletin No. 57 (Publication Number 96-100), June 1996. To obtain a copy, call the toll-free number or access the Internet at www.cdc.gov/niosh/homicide.html.

Callers may also use the toll-free number to find a directory of topics of publications and databases that may be ordered. Recorded summaries that provide overviews and relevant statistics about selected topics are also available. Use the automated fax information service to receive documents within fifteen minutes. Technical information specialists may also be reached at this number from 9:00 a.m. to 4:00 p.m. Eastern time, Monday through Friday. Callers may also learn about NIOSH training resources or request a NIOSH workplace health hazard evaluation. Access the Internet at www.cdc.gov/niosh/homepage.html.

Department of Justice
National Institute of Justice
National Criminal Justice Reference Service
Bureau of Justice Assistance Clearinghouse (BJAC)
P.O. Box 6000
Rockville, MD 20849-6000
(800) 851-3420

Calling the toll-free number offers several information options including a fax-on-demand service for documents, being able to speak with a specialist, or learning about how to access an electronic newsletter through their website and e-mail address.

The caller can also learn about their Research and Information Center, located in Rockville, Maryland. BJAC also has a catalog of National Institute of Justice documents. Many of the documents included in the catalog pertain to workplace violence—for example, *Violence and Theft in the Workplace, The Cycle of Violence, Psychoactive Substances and Violence,* and *Crime Prevention through Environmental Design in Parking Facilities*. Access the website at www.ncjrs.org.

Department of Labor
Occupational Safety and Health Administration (OSHA)
200 Constitution Avenue NW, Room N3107

Washington, DC 20210
General information: (202) 219-8031
Publications: (202) 219-4667

OSHA has various publications, standards, technical assistance, and compliance tools to help you, and offers extensive assistance through its many safety and health programs: workplace consultation, voluntary protection programs, grants, strategic partnerships, state plans, training, and education. Guidance such as OSHA's Safety and Health Management Program Guidelines identify elements that are critical to the development of a successful safety and health management system. This and other information are available on OSHA's website at www.osha.gov.

For a free copy of OSHA publications, send a self-addressed mailing label to this address: OSHA Publications Office, P.O. Box 37535, Washington, DC 20013-7535; send a request by fax to (202) 693-2498; or call (202) 693-1888.

To file a complaint by phone; report an emergency; or get OSHA advice, assistance, or products, contact your nearest OSHA office under the "U.S. Department of Labor" listing in your phone book, or call (800) 321-OSHA (6742). The teletypewriter (TTY) number is (877) 889-5627.

To file a complaint online or obtain more information on OSHA federal and state programs, visit OSHA's website.

Women's Bureau
200 Constitution Avenue NW
Washington, DC 20210
(202) 219-6665

The Women's Bureau has issued *Domestic Violence: A Workplace Issue*, Document Number 96-3.

Nongovernment Resources

American Psychiatric Association (APA)
Division of Public Affairs
1400 K Street NW
Washington, DC 20005

The APA publishes a free fact sheet, *Violence and Mental Illness*, Document Number 6109. To obtain a copy, call the APA's fast fax automatic document retrieval service at (888) 267-5400 or access the Internet at www.psych.org/ (listed under Resources for the General Public, Fact Sheet Series).

American Psychological Association (APA)
1200 17th Street NW
Washington, DC 20036
(202) 955-7600

Information on violence is available on APA's website at www.apa.org/.

International Association of Chiefs of Police (IACP)
515 North Washington Street
Alexandria, VA 22314-2357

The IACP has published a booklet *Combating Workplace Violence: Guidelines for Employers and Law Enforcement*. To obtain a copy, write to the IACP at the address above.

International Critical Incident Stress Foundation
10176 Baltimore National Pike, Unit 201
Ellicott City, MD 21042
(410) 750-9600

The International Critical Incident Stress Foundation provides information and training on critical incident stress management.

National Crime Prevention Council (NCPC)
1700 K Street NW, Suite 618
Washington, DC 20006
(202) 466-6272

NCPC provides information on the prevention of crime and violence.

National Domestic Violence Hotline
(800) 799-SAFE or (800) 787-3224 (TTY)

This nationwide hotline offers crisis intervention, problem-solving skills, information, and referral to service agency providers.

National Organization for Victim Assistance (NOVA)
1757 Park Road NW
Washington, DC 20010
(202) TRY-NOVA

NOVA refers callers to local victim assistance organizations.

National Victims' Center
P.O. Box 588
Arlington, VA 22216
(800) FYI-CALL

The National Victims' Center provides information and referrals to local victim assistance organizations.

Partnership against Violence Network (PAVNET)
www.pavnet.org

PAVNET is a clearinghouse with over five hundred entries on violence. Information in PAVNET includes funding grants, research projects, grassroots efforts to address violence, and curriculum development.

Government and nongovernment organizations addressing the subject of violence are listed.

GHR Training Solutions
7467 Granville Drive
Tamarac, FL 33321
(954) 720-1512
Solutions@GHR-Training.com

Training and speaking services provided by Don and Sheryl Grimme. Websites include www.GHR-Training.com, www.Workplace-Violence-HQ.com, and www.Employee-Retention-HQ.com.

Bibliography

Albrecht, S. *Fear and Violence on the Job: Prevention Solutions for the Dangerous Workplace.* Durham, NC: Carolina Academic Press, 1997.

Allcorn, S., and M. Diamond. *Anger in the Workplace: Understanding the Causes of Aggression and Violence.* Westport, CT: Quorum Books, 1994.

American Institute on Domestic Violence. www.aidv-usa.com/.

Andersson, L. M., and C. M. Pearson. "Tit for Tat? The Spiraling Effect of Incivility in the Workplace." *Academy of Management Review* 24, no. 3 (1999): 452–71.

Arbury, S. "Workplace Violence: Training Young Workers in Preventative Strategies." *NFIB Business Toolbox*, March 4, 2005.

Booher, D. "Resolving Conflict without Punching Someone Out." *Office World News* 27 (1999): 1–2.

Bowman, J. S., and C. J. Zigmond. "State Government Response to Workplace Violence." *Public Personnel Management Journal* 26, no. 2 (1997): 289–300.

Braverman, M. "Seven Steps to Preventing Workplace Violence." In *Preventing Workplace Violence: A Guide for Employers and Practitioners.* Thousand Oaks, CA: Sage, 1999.

Chavez, L. J. "Workplace Violence 101." Critical Incident Associates. www.workplace-violence.com/.

Clay, R. "Securing the Workplace: Are Our Fears Misplaced?" *Monitor on Psychology* 31, no. 9 (October 2000).

Currall, S. C., R. A. Friedmann, S. T. Tidd, and J. C. Tsai. "What Goes Around Comes Around: The Impact of Personal Conflict Style on Work." *International Journal of Conflict Management* 11, no. 1 (2000): 32–55.

Danforth, K. D. "Reading Reasonableness out of the ADA: Responding to Threats by Employees with Mental Illness Following Palmer." *Virginia Law Review* 85, no. 4 (1999): 661–95.

de Becker, G. *The Gift of Fear.* New York: Dell, 1997.

Denenberg, T. S., R. V. Denenberg, M. Braverman, and S. Braverman. "Dispute Resolution and Workplace Violence." *Dispute Resolution Journal* (January–March 1996). www.wps.org/pubs/dispute-resolution.html.

Farrah, C. "Violence in the Workplace and Ergonomic Prevention." *Work* 14, no. 2 (2000): 159.

Federal Bureau of Investigation. *Workplace Violence: Issues in Response.* Quantico, VA: FBI Academy, 2004. www.fbi.gov/publications/violence.pdf.

Flannery, R. *Violence in the Workplace.* New York: Crossroad Publishing, 1995.

Freiberg, P. "Bullying in the Workplace Is a Violence Warning Sign." *Monitor on Psychology* 29, no. 7 (July 1998).

Gedman, C. M. "Workplace Violence and Domestic Violence: A Proactive Approach." *Journal of Healthcare Protection Management* 14 (1998): 45–54.

Ginn, G. O., and L. J. Henry. "Addressing Workplace Violence from a Health Management Perspective." *Advanced Management Journal* 67, no. 4 (2002): 4.

Grimme, D., and S. Grimme. *The New Manager's Tool Kit.* New York: AMACOM Books, 2008.

Gurchiek, K. "Workplace Violence Is on the Upswing, Say HR Leaders." *HR Magazine* (July 2005). newsmanager.commpartners.com/hrma/issues/2005-05-25/12.html.

Howard, J. L. "Workplace Violence in Organizations: An Exploratory Study of Organizational Prevention Techniques." *Employee Responsibilities and Rights Journal* 13, no. 2 (2001): 57–75.

Jacob, I. G. "Defusing the Explosive Worker." *Occupational Health and Safety* 73, no. 1 (2004): 56–60.

Kelleher, M. D. *New Arenas for Violence: Homicide in the American Workplace.* Westport, CT: Praeger, 1996.

Kinney, J. A. *Breaking Point: The Workplace Violence Epidemic and What to Do About It.* Chicago: National Safe Workplace Institute, 1993.

Labig, C. E. *Preventing Violence in the Workplace.* New York: AMACOM Books, 1995.

McClure, L. F. *Anger and conflict in the workplace.* Manassas Park, VA: Impact Publications, 2000.

———. *Risky Business: Managing Employee Violence in the Workplace.* Binghamton, NY: Haworth Press, 1996.

National Institute for Occupational Safety and Health. "Occupational Violence." www.cdc.gov/niosh/topics/violence/.

———. "Violence in the Workplace." www.cdc.gov/niosh/violcont.html.

Nelson, Bob. *1001 Ways to Energize Employees.* New York: Workman Publishing, 1997.

———. *1001 Ways to Reward Employees.* New York: Workman Publishing, 1994.

Peek-Asa, C., C. Casteel, L. Mineschian, R. J. Erickson, and J. F. Kraus. "Compliance to a Workplace Violence Prevention Program in Small Businesses." *American Journal of Preventive Medicine* 26, no. 4 (May 2004): 276–83.

Philpott, D., and S. Einstein. *The Integrated Physical Security Handbook,* Homeland Defense Journal, 2006.

Rogers, K. A., and D. Chappell. *Preventing and Responding to Violence at Work.* Geneva: International Labor Office, 2003.

"Seung-Hui Cho." en.wikipedia.org/wiki/Seung-Hui_Cho.

Tyme, J. *Workplace Violence Awareness and Prevention FAQs, Facts, and Answers.* 2004.

U.S. Department of Justice. Bureau of Labor Statistics. "Violence and Theft in the Workplace." www.ojp.usdoj.gov/bjs/pub/press/thefwork.pr.

———. "Workplace Violence, 1992–96." www.ojp.usdoj.gov/bjs/abstract/wv96.htm.

U.S. Department of Labor. Occupational Safety and Health Administration. *Preventing Workplace Violence.* 1999.

———. "Safety and Health Topics: Workplace Violence." www.osha.gov/SLTC/workplaceviolence/index.html.

U.S. Office of Personnel Management. *Dealing with Workplace Violence: A Guide for Agency Planners.* February 1998. www.opm.gov/employment_and_benefits/worklife/officialdocuments/handbooksguides/workplaceviolence/full.pdf.

Ventrice, C. *Make Their Day! Employee Retention That Works.* 2nd ed. San Francisco: Berrett-Koehler, 2009.

About the Authors

Don Philpott has published over five thousand articles in newspapers and magazines in the United States and the United Kingdom, and has written more than ninety books on a wide range of subjects, including *Is America Safe* (2006), *The Interrated Physical Security Handbook* (2006), and *The Wounded Warrior Handbook* (2008).

Don Grimme is the president of GHR Training Solutions, a nationwide "workplace people solutions" consulting firm, and coauthor of the groundbreaking book on managing people in today's workplace, *The New Manager's Tool Kit* (2008). His website (www.Workplace-Violence-HQ.com) and articles are among the most frequently quoted resources on the subject.